SQL BY EXAMPLE

SQL BY EXAMPLE

JOHN RUSSO

MP **MOMENTUM** PRESS
ENGINEERING

MOMENTUM PRESS, LLC, NEW YORK

SQL By Example

Copyright © Momentum Press®, LLC, 2019.

First published by Momentum Press®, LLC
222 East 46th Street, New York, NY 10017
www.momentumpress.net

ISBN-13: 978-1-94561-262-6 (print)
ISBN-13: 978-1-94561-263-3 (e-book)

Momentum Press Computer Science Collection

Cover and interior design by Exeter Premedia Services Private Ltd., Chennai, India

10 9 8 7 6 5 4 3 2 1

Printed in the United States of America

This book is dedicated to my wife Kim and children Sara, Sam and Sophie. Without their support and understanding, it would not have been written. I'd also like to thank my parents for giving me a good education to get started on this career. Finally, I'd like to also dedicate this to my good friend and neurosurgeon, the late Dr. John Shillito. Without his skilled work so many years ago I would not have had all that I have today.

ABSTRACT

SQL by Example uses one case study to teach the reader basic structured query language (SQL) skills. The author has tested the case study in the classroom with thousands of students. While other SQL texts tend to use examples from many different data sets, the author has found that once students get used to one case study, they learn the material at a much faster rate. The text begins with an introduction to the case study and trains the reader to think like the query processing engine for a relational database management system. Once the reader has a grasp of the case study then SQL programming constructs are introduced with examples from the case study. In order to reinforce concepts, each chapter has several exercises with solutions provided on the book's website. SQL by Example is designed both for those who have never worked with SQL as well as those with some experience. It is modular in that each chapter can be approached individually or as part of a sequence, giving the reader flexibility in the way that they learn or refresh concepts. This also makes the book a great reference to refer back to once the reader is honing his or her SQL skills on the job.

KEYWORDS

query language; query; RDBMS; relation database management systems; SQL; Structured query language; table

CONTENTS

LIST OF FIGURES

LIST OF TABLES

ACKNOWLEDGMENTS

I would first like to thank the thousands of students who have successfully used the Shore to Shore Shipping case study over the years. Through their feedback, the case study has been refined and made even more useful.

I would also like to thank my former institution, Wentworth Institute of Technology, as well as my current college, Landmark College, for the support during the writing of this book. I would also like to thank my mentor and friend, Meggin McIntosh who gave me invaluable guidance to bring this project to completion. In addition, I would like to thank my mentor and friend, Monte Unger, who helped me to realize my desire to write.

INTRODUCTION

The study of relational database management systems is a core part of computer science education. In the workplace, you will find that having knowledge of database management systems and how to extract data from such systems is beneficial for many different job functions. This book does not cover the design of databases, but rather covers basic syntax to retrieve data from a database management system. If you are a student in computer science, this text will be an excellent companion to a text on database design. If you are a professional looking to learn SQL or expand your skills, this text will provide you with the groundwork necessary to expand your skills and begin learning SQL.

KEY FEATURES

1. Unified Case Study
    While there are many SQL books on the market today, most use multiple datasets to teach concepts. Through 20 years of teaching database management systems and SQL, the author has found that students learn best by being taught how to think like the database management system's query processor. As such, the text starts off with an overview of the case study as well as many queries written out in long form, not using the language at this point. Once students have gained familiarity with the case study they are then introduced to the language in small bites, focusing on one particular aspect or clause of the select statement. All examples in the book can be run using MySQL or another relational database management system with the scripts provided on the book's website.
2. On Your Own Exercises
    Each chapter has a series of on your exercises with solutions provided on the book's website. The exercises are not at the back of the chapter but occur whenever the coverage of one topic is finished

before moving on to the next topic. It is important for students to use these as way to check on their understanding of the concepts just introduced.

3. Modular

   SQL by Example has been designed to be modular in nature. Readers who have had some introduction to SQL can quickly read through the first chapter and then jump to any chapter where they feel a need to refresh their skills.

4. RDBMS Agnostic

   As much as possible, the text has been designed to be used with any relational database management system.

PATHWAYS OF LEARNING

As mentioned earlier, all readers should start with Chapter 1 in order to gain a firm understanding of the case study. There are then multiple pathways of learning. Readers without any SQL experience should read the text sequentially. More experienced readers can skip to sections of interest based on what skills they need to expand. The following table is a logical grouping of chapters.

Topic	Chapters
Basic SQL syntax	2 and 3
Joining tables	4 and 5
Sub-queries	6
Grouping	7

SCRIPTS AND SOLUTION FILES

The scripts for the case study as well as solutions to the on your own exercises and scripts to run example queries can be found at www.profrusso.com/SQL_BY_EXAMPLE. Also, instructions for loading the scripts can be found here.

CHAPTER 1

THE SHORE TO SHORE SHIPPING CASE STUDY

1.1 OVERVIEW

In this chapter, I will first introduce a case study that we will use through-out our discussion of SQL. I have designed this case study after numer-ous iterations of teaching SQL and have found that students learn best by using one set of tables with which they become very familiar. Once the case study has been presented, we will then go through several sample queries by hand. The objective of this is to learn to think through queries before writing the actual SQL. We will then move on to a discussion of SQL syntax and present some examples from the case study.

1.2 OBJECTIVES

- Introduce the Shore to Shore Shipping Company case study
- Discuss thinking through queries
- Discuss problem solving using relational databases

1.3 THE SHORE TO SHORE SHIPPING COMPANY CASE STUDY

The Shore to Shore Shipping Company is a small merchant marine opera-tion that wishes to keep track of ships, ship manufacturers, shipments, and ship captains. The company operates all over the world and currently has several hundred ships. Because the company is growing, management has decided to develop a database management system to produce shipment manifests as well as management reports. Management has determined that there are four types of data that must be maintained and reported on:

1. Ship
   (a) Each ship has a ship number, class, capacity, date of purchase and manufacturer ID.
   (b) Each ship manufacturer has a manufacturer ID, name, city, state, representative ID and a bidding preference.
2. Captain
   - Each captain has an ID, a first name, last name, license grade and a date of birth.
3. Item
   - Every item that is shipped has an item number, a type, a description and a weight.
4. Shipment
   When a shipment is sent out, a shipment manifest is generated, as shown in Figure 1.1.

The shipment manifest is composed of three parts, each of which contains unique information.

(a) The heading contains the shipment id, order date, origin, and destination, expected date of arrival, ship number and captain.
(b) The body of the manifest contains line items, which represent a component of the shipment. Each line contains an item number, type, description, weight and quantity. The total weight is calculated by multiplying the weight by the quantity.

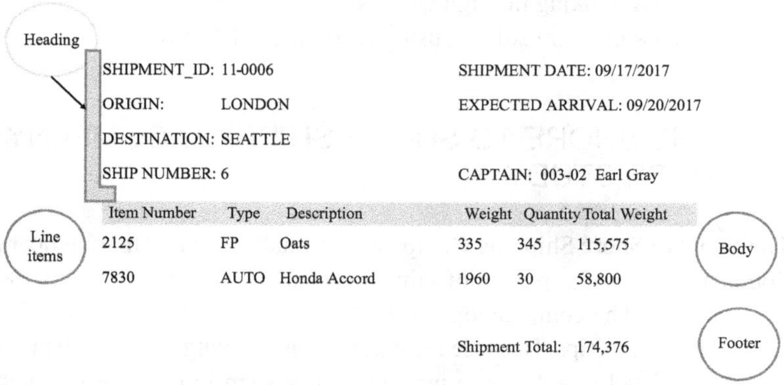

Figure 1.1. Shipment manifest.

(c) The footing of the manifest contains the total weight for the entire shipment. This is compared against the capacity of the ship to ensure that a ship is not overloaded.

Based upon the shipment manifest, the following additional information must be stored in the database:

(a) For every shipment, the shipment id, date that the shipment left port, the origin, destination, ship number and captain. Additional information about the captain is stored with the captain information. The expected arrival date is not stored but is calculated based upon the origin and destination. Although it is not shown on the shipment manifest, the arrival date of the shipment is recorded and stored in the database when it arrives at its destination.

(b) For each line item, the shipment id, item number and quantity. The type, description and weight are stored with the item information. The total weight is not stored, since it can be calculated from the weight and the quantity.

(c) The shipment total weight is not stored in the database. It can be calculated whenever it is needed for a report or query.

Figures 1.2 to 1.8 show sample data for Shore to Shore. Let's take a look around and explore the data a little bit. Once you have a thorough

capt_id	license_grade	fname	lname	dob
001-01	3	Robert	Sourchie	1945-05-01
001-23	1	Cliff	Walker	1972-02-01
001-24	1	John	Smith	1957-01-12
001-25	2	Mark	Smith	1973-05-17
002-14	2	Sal	Levine	1956-02-20
002-15	1	Henry	Moore	1957-01-15
003-01	3	James	Westmoreland	1972-02-12
003-02	1	Earl	Gray	1965-03-17
004-01	2	Otheno	Vollage	1962-11-16
004-02	1	Marcia	Nesmith	1957-05-01
004-03	1	Paul	Rice	1977-09-10
011-11	2	Phillip	Levinchuck	1962-03-02

Figure 1.2. The captain table.

MANUFACTURER

manufacturer_id	name	city	state
210	United ship Builders	Bath	ME
211	General ship Builders	San Diego	CA
212	Master Dynamics	Bridgeport	CT
213	Asia West ship Builders	Hong Kong	NULL
214	Pacific ship Builders	Fairbanks	AK
215	Best Industries	Seattle	WA
216	Union Corp	Buffalo	NY

Figure 1.3. The manufacturer table.

SHIP

ship_no	class	capacity	purch_date	manufacturer_id
1	1	100000.00	1965-01-25	212
10	3	20000.00	1976-03-15	210
11	2	50000.00	1971-01-30	210
16	2	75000.00	1975-11-01	215
25	3	15000.00	1979-11-02	213
35	2	55000.00	1989-12-01	211
37	1	250000.00	1990-12-02	216
39	1	500000.00	1991-12-03	211
5	1	120000.00	1969-01-20	212
6	1	500000.00	1969-03-07	212

Figure 1.4. The ship table.

understanding of the data, we will begin to look at how the tables are related and how information can be obtained by combining tables. But first, let's begin by examining each table, its columns and our sample data.

1.4 CAPTAIN

We have included 12 rows in our table. Each captain has an ID that uniquely identifies him or her. Notice that this ID column is named Capt_ID and is the left most column in the table. The first captain has an ID of 001-01 and the last captain in the table has an ID of 011-11. Each captain also has a license grade that is used to determine the class of ship that he

ITEM

item_no	item_type	description	weight
2101	FP	Beans	500.00
2109	FP	Corn Meal	200.00
2123	FP	Rice	300.00
2125	FP	Oats	335.00
3212	BL	Cement	2000.00
3223	BL	Concrete Forms	500.00
3297	BL	Steel Beam	2000.00
3299	BL	Small Steel Plate	750.00
4521	WP	5/8" Plywood - 200 sheets/pallet	800.00
4532	WP	Beam	100.00
4533	WP	2X4X8 Pine Boards	250.00
4534	WP	3/4" Plywood - 200 sheets/pallet	1200.00
7821	AUTO	Toyota Camry	2000.00
7823	AUTO	Mercury Sable	2500.00
7829	AUTO	Mercedes	2550.00
7830	AUTO	Honda Accord	1960.00

Figure 1.5. The item table.

SHIPMENT

shipment_id	ship_no	capt_id	shipment_date	origin	destination	arrival_date
09-0001	25	001-25	2016-03-12	SEATTLE	BOSTON	2016-03-19
09-0002	1	004-03	2016-04-15	BOSTON	SINGAPORE	2016-04-20
09-0003	11	003-01	2016-06-01	BRAZIL	BOSTON	2016-06-07
09-0004	5	002-14	2016-07-10	LONDON	SEATTLE	2016-07-22
09-0005	1	002-15	2016-09-19	BOSTON	BRAZIL	2016-09-23
10-0001	1	001-23	2017-01-15	BOSTON	LONDON	2017-01-21
10-0002	5	001-01	2017-01-15	SEATTLE	LONDON	2017-01-21
10-0003	11	002-14	2017-01-18	BOSTON	LONDON	2017-01-30
10-0004	39	001-24	2017-03-13	BOSTON	LONDON	2017-03-18
11-0001	39	002-15	2018-06-10	BOSTON	BRAZIL	2018-06-14
11-0002	37	004-01	2018-07-15	BRAZIL	BOSTON	2018-07-19
11-0003	10	003-01	2018-08-20	BOSTON	SEATTLE	2018-08-31
11-0004	16	001-24	2018-09-01	SEATTLE	LONDON	2018-09-14
11-0005	5	004-02	2018-09-15	BOSTON	SEATTLE	2018-09-23
11-0006	6	003-02	2018-09-17	LONDON	SEATTLE	2018-09-28

Figure 1.6. The shipment table.

or she can pilot. This column is called License_Grade. We can look across the table from Capt_ID to License_Grade and determine that the captain with an ID of 002-14 has a license grade of 2. Since we also want to keep

DISTANCE

origin	destination	miles	days
BOSTON	BRAZIL	2500.00	4
BOSTON	LONDON	3000.00	5
BOSTON	SEATTLE	6000.00	7
BOSTON	SINGAPORE	5000.00	5
BRAZIL	BOSTON	2600.00	5
LONDON	BOSTON	3000.00	5
LONDON	SEATTLE	9000.00	12
SEATTLE	BOSTON	6000.00	7
SEATTLE	LONDON	9000.00	12
SINGAPORE	BOSTON	5000.00	5

Figure 1.7. The distance table.

track of a captain's name, we have two columns to store the captain's first name (Fname) and last name (Lname). Looking again to our data, you can see that captain 004-02 is named Marcia Nesmith. Finally, we wish to store the date of birth for each captain in a column named DOB. Marcia Nesmith's date of birth is May 1, 1957.

1.4.1 ON YOUR OWN EXERCISES

Now, just to make sure that you understand the data in the table, answer the following review questions. We are not asking you to write SQL queries, but rather to just answer the questions by looking at the captain table.

1.1 What is the license grade of OthenoVollage?
1.2 Which captain is the oldest and what is his or her license grade and captain ID?
1.3 How many captains have a license grade of 1?
1.4 How many captains were born after 1970?

SHIPMENT_LINE

shipment_id	item_no	quantity
09-0001	3223	100.00
09-0001	3297	87.00
09-0001	3299	34.00
09-0002	3212	100.00
09-0002	3223	50.00
09-0003	2101	432.00
09-0003	2109	1000.00
09-0003	2123	34.00
09-0003	2125	200.00
09-0004	3212	10.00
09-0004	3223	5.00
09-0005	3297	42.00
09-0005	7821	5.00
09-0005	7823	45.00
10-0001	7821	10.00
10-0001	7829	3.00
10-0001	7830	100.00
10-0002	4521	100.00
10-0002	4532	100.00

Figure 1.8a. The shipment_line table (part 1 of 2).

shipment_id	item_no	quantity
10-0002	4533	1000.00
10-0003	4521	100.00
10-0003	4534	300.00
10-0004	2101	1000.00
10-0004	2109	800.00
10-0004	2125	56.00
11-0001	4521	10.00
11-0001	4532	100.00
11-0002	4533	100.00
11-0002	4534	15.00
11-0003	7829	1000.00
11-0004	3223	150.00
11-0004	3297	10.00
11-0005	2101	100.00
11-0005	2109	1000.00
11-0006	2125	345.00
11-0006	7830	30.00

Figure 1.8b. The shipment_line table (part 2 of 2).

1.5 MANUFACTURER

There are seven manufacturers in our table, each with a unique manufacturer ID numbered from 210 to 216. Manufacturer 212 is named Master Dynamics and is located in Bridgeport, Connecticut.

1.6 SHIP

There are also 10 ships in our ship table. Each ship has a unique ship number, class, capacity (in pounds), purchase date, and manufacturer ID. For example, ship number 11 is a class 2 ship with a capacity of 50,000 pounds. It was purchased on January 30, 1971 and was manufactured by manufacturer ID 210 (United Ship Builders).

Notice that we do not store specific information about the manufacturer in the ship table. This information is stored separately in the manufacturer table. Later on, you will learn about joining tables together to perform multitable queries. In order to help you to understand this better, let's try gathering some information from both the ship and manufacturer table.

1.6.1 EXAMPLE QUERIES

Example 1.1 Which manufacturer built ship number 37?

Solution:
First, we will look in the ship table. The manufacturer ID for ship number 37 is 216. Next, look at the manufacturer table.
    Manufacturer ID 216 is Union Corp.

Example 1.2 Which ships were built by General Ship Builders?

Solution:
Since the ship table does not contain the name of the manufacturer, but only the manufacturer ID, we need to look at the manufacturer table first to find the ID for General Ship Builders, which is 211. Next, we can examine the ship table and see that ships 35 and 39 have a manufacturer ID of 211.

Example 1.3 List all the different classes of ships that were built by manufacturers located in California (State = CA):

Solution:
For this query, we simply want to list the distinct combinations of classes. Since we do not have specific information about the manufacturer in the ship table, we must join both tables together. First, let's look at the manufacturer table. We can see that the only manufacturer in California is General Ship Builders. The manufacturer ID is 211. Next, let's look at the ship table. We can see that ships 35 and 39 both have 211 as the manufacturer ID. Notice that ship 35 has a class of 2 and ship 39 has a class of 1. Therefore, all manufacturers in California build class 1 and class 2 ships.

1.6.2 ON YOUR OWN EXERCISES

For each exercise, write out the answer as well as how you obtained the result

- 2.1 List the manufacturers of all class 2 ships.
- 2.2 List the manufacturers of all ships with a capacity of 100,000 pounds or more.
- 2.3 List all ships purchased after 1975 and manufactured in another country.
- 2.4 List any manufacturers who did not sell a ship to Shore to Shore. (Hint: make a list of all manufacturer IDS in the ship table and then list all manufacturers who are not in that list.)

1.7 ITEM

There are 16 items, each with a unique item number. Let's look at item 2123, which is of type FP and has a description of Rice. Its weight is 300 pounds for one unit. The item types are used to differentiate the different categories of items. For example, FP is short for food products, BL for building materials, and so on.

1.8 DISTANCE

The Distance table is used to keep track of the distance between any given origin and destination. Looking at the distance table, you can see that the distance between Boston and Brazil is 2,500 miles and takes four days. The number of days is used to calculate an estimate of the arrival date.

1.9 SHIPMENT

The shipment table is used to store information on each individual shipment such as the number of the ship, the captain, origin and destination. The arrival date is entered into the shipment table after the shipment has arrived at its destination. Each shipment is identified by a unique shipment ID. Let's look at shipment 11-0005, which is going from Boston to Seattle. The shipment left port on September 15, 2018 and arrived on the September 23, 2018. It was shipped using ship number 05. The captain ID is 004-02. A quick glance over at the captain table tells us that the captain's name is Marcia Nesmith. We might be curious to see when this shipment is expected to arrive. If we look at the Distance table, we can see that Boston to Seattle normally takes seven days. This shipment should have arrived on September 22, 2018. Management reports could be generated from calculations such as this to flag problems.

Since the Shipment table can be linked to the Ship table by ship_no, the Captain table by capt_id and the Distance table by origin and destination, we can find out a lot of useful information about each shipment based upon information contained in the other tables. Once again, we will present several queries and explain how to generate the results. Of course, you will also have the opportunity to explore the tables on your own.

1.9.1 EXAMPLE QUERIES:

Example 2.1 List all shipments that originated in Boston.

Solution:
We can examine the origin column and determine that eight shipments originated in Boston: 09-0002, 09-0005, 10-0001, 10-0003, 10-0004, 11-0001, 11-0003, 11-0005

Example 2.2 List all shipments that require more than five days of travel.

Solution:
First, we need to examine the Distance table and find all combinations of origin and destination that have a value greater than five in the days column.

We can see that the following combinations meet this requirement:

Origin	Destination
BOSTON	SEATTLE
LONDON	SEATTLE
SEATTLE	BOSTON
SEATTLE	LONDON

Next, let's look at the Shipment table and find all shipments that have any Origin and Destination combinations shown in the preceding table. We can see that shipments 11-0003 and 11-0005 go from Boston to Seattle, shipments 09-0004 and 11-0006 go from London to Seattle, shipments 10-0002 and 11-0004 go from Seattle to London. Shipment 09-0001 goes from Seattle to Boston. Therefore, the results of our query are the following shipments:

09-0001
09-0004
10-0002
11-0003
11-0004
11-0005
11-0006

Example 2.3 List all shipments that had John Smith as the captain.

Solution:

Since the shipment table only contains the captain ID, we need to first look up the captain ID for John Smith in the Captain table. His ID is 001-24. Now, let's look back at the shipment table. We can see that he was the captain for shipment 10-0004 and shipment 11-0004.

Example 2.4 List all shipments that were carried by a ship manufactured by General Ship Builders.

Solution:
This is a bit more complicated query and will require two steps.
    The first step is to determine the ship numbers for all ships manufactured by General Ship Builders. This is the same query as example 1.2. The result of example 1.2 was ship 35 and 39.
    The next step is to look at the Shipment table and find all shipments with a ship number of 35 or 39. Upon careful examination, we determine that shipments 10-0004 and 11-0001 were carried by ship number 39.

1.9.2   ON YOUR OWN EXERCISES

For each exercise, write out the answer as well as how you obtained the result.

3.1 List all shipments that were greater than 3,000 miles.
3.2 List all shipments that were greater than 3,000 miles and had Sal Levine as the captain.
3.3 Find the total number of shipments that originated in Boston.

3.4 List all shipments that originated in Boston and were carried by ships built by General Ship Builders.

3.5 (Advanced) List all the shipments that arrived late. (Hint: only look at shipments with an arrival date, assume that a blank arrival date means that the shipment has not arrived yet. The expected arrival date can be calculated by adding the days from the distance table to the shipment date.)

1.10   SHIPMENT_LINE

Because each shipment contains several items, a separate table is needed to store each line item on the manifest. When you first glance at the shipment manifest, you might think that it makes more sense to keep the line item information in the shipment table. Figure 1.9 shows us what the table design would look like with these changes for a subset of the data.

This table contains the same information as the Shipment and Shipment_Line tables, except that all the information is stored in one table. For example, shipment ID 09-0003 contains an entry for 100 of item number 2125 and 1000 of item number 2109. While this approach might seem more effective, the table is more complicated and could not be practically implemented without duplicating data. One issue is how much room to allow for the multiple entries? What do you do if there are more order lines than you initially anticipated? As you study database management systems, you will learn about proper table design. One of the fundamental precepts of database management systems is to avoid duplication of data.

Let's take a look at the shipment line table. There is one row for each item contained in a shipment. This row contains the shipment ID, item number and quantity. For example, shipment ID 09-0002 contains 100 of item number 3212 and 50 of item number 3223. Now, let's take a look at some queries to see how we can use this table.

1.10.1 Example Queries

Example 3.1 List all shipments that contained item number 3223

Solution:
We can look at the item_no column and determine that the following shipments contained item 3223: 09-0001, 09-0002, 09-0004, 11-0004

Example 3.2 List all shipments that contain food products (type=FP).

Solution:
First, we need to determine all item numbers of items that are type FP.

SHIPMENT_ID	SHIP_NO	CAPT_ID	SHIPMENT_DATE	ORIGIN	DESTINATION	ARRIVAL_DATE	ITEM_NO	QUANTITY
09-0001	25	001-25	March 12, 2016	SEATTLE	BOSTON	March 19, 2016	3223	100
							3297	87
							3299	34
09-0002	1	004-03	April 15, 2016	BOSTON	SINGAPORE	April 20, 2016	3212	100
							3223	50
09-0003	11	003-01	June 01, 2016	BRAZIL	BOSTON	June 07, 2016	2101	432
							2109	1000
							2123	34
							2125	100
09-0004	5	002-14	July 10, 2016	LONDON	SEATTLE	July 22, 2016	3212	10
							3223	5
09-0005	1	002-15	September 19, 2016	BOSTON	BRAZIL	September 23, 2016	3297	42
							7821	5
							7823	45
10-0001	1	001-23	January 15, 2017	BOSTON	LONDON	January 21, 2017	7821	10
							7829	3
							7830	100

Figure 1.9. Line items included in shipment table.

Upon examination of the Item table, we find that item numbers 2101, 2109, 2123, and 2125 are of this type.

Next, looking at the Item_no column of the Shipment_Line table, we find that shipment 10-0004 contains items 2101, 2109, and 2125. Shipment 11-0005 contains items 2101 and 2109. Shipment 11-0006 contains only 2125 and shipment 09-0003 contains all of the items that are of type food product.

Example 3.3 List all shipments that contain building materials (Type=BL) and were shipped on a ship manufactured by Best Industries.

Solution:

Whenever you encounter a fairly complex problem, it is best to break it down into smaller subproblems and look for problems which you have seen before. In this case, our first subproblem would be to determine the shipment numbers of all shipments that carried building materials. This is exactly the same problem as example 3.2, except we are looking for shipments that contain building materials instead of food products. By examining the Item and the Shipment_Line tables, we determine that shipments 09-0001, 09-0002, 09-0004, 09-0005, and 11-0004 contained building materials. Notice that the shipment_line table does not contain any information about the ship other than the ship number. We must go to the ship table to determine which ships were manufactured by Best Industries. This query is the same as example query 2.2, except we are looking for all ships manufactured by Best Industries. Since the ship table does not contain the name of the manufacturer, but only the manufacturer ID, we need to look at the manufacturer table first to find the ID for Best Industries, which is 215. Next, we can examine the ship table and see that ship number 16 has a manufacturers ID of 215.

Now, armed with our list of shipments which contain building materials and our knowledge that ship number 16 was built by Best Industries, we can now examine the shipment table.

Ship number 16 carried shipment 11-0004, which is in our list of shipments that contain building materials.

We can also represent this graphically. As you go through the textbook and learn to develop queries, it is often easier to map out the queries graphically, as in Figure 1.10.

1.10.2 ON YOUR OWN EXERCISES

4.1 List all shipments that contained automobiles (Type = AUTO)

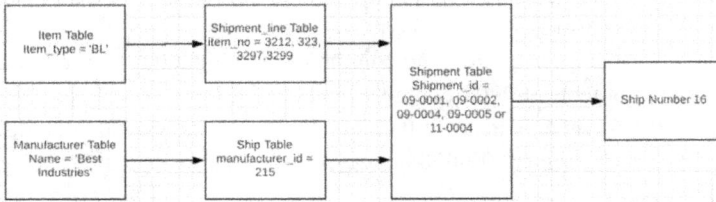

Figure 1.10. Graphical map of a query.

4.2 List all shipments that had John Smith as the captain and contained building materials.

4.3 List the total weight for shipment number 09-0001.

4.4 Find the shipment that weighed the most.

1.11 PROBLEM SOLVING USING DATABASE MANAGEMENT SYSTEMS

Now that we have fully described each of the tables in the Shore to Shore case study, we can begin to think about some practical ways in which the data would be useful to the organization. Databases are used in most businesses not just to store information and produce reports, invoices and other documents, but also to provide management with a means of keeping the organization on target with organizational goals. Let's examine one scenario in which the database can be used to assist management. We will also give you an exercise to try on your own.

The management of Shore to Shore has noticed that there is a problem with shipments arriving late. Each month, they would like a report to show shipments that arrived late. A sample report is shown in Figure 1.11.

In order to produce this report, we must think about what information we are going to need and where it will come from:

1. Heading
   The reporting period will be entered by the user, whether it is a computer operator running the report or a manager who might want to view it on the screen. The reporting period will be used to determine what records to include in the detail section of the report.

2. Body
   The following information contained in the body of the report will come directly from the corresponding table as shown in Figure 1.12.

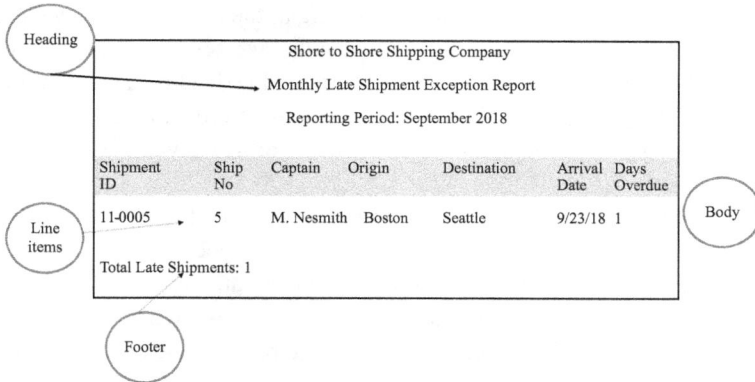

Figure 1.11. Sample report.

Data element	Table	Column
Shipment ID	Shipment	SHIPMENT_ID
Ship no	Shipment	SHIP_NO
Captain	Captain	FIRSTNAME
		LASTNAME
Origin	Shipment	ORIGIN
Destination	Shipment	DESTINATION
Arrival date	Shipment	ARRIVAL_DATE
Days overdue	Shipment	Calculated
	Distance	

Figure 1.12. Data elements for report.

As you can see, most of the information in the body is directly obtained from the shipment table except for the following:

Captain's Name

This data element is obtained by finding the captain ID for the overdue shipment and then looking up the corresponding last name and first name in the CAPTAIN table.

Days Overdue

In order to determine if a shipment is overdue, we first must calculate the expected arrival date and compare this to the actual arrival date. The expected arrival date is calculated by adding the number of days that the shipment should normally take to the shipment date. The number of days that the shipment should take is found in the distance table. In our sample report, the shipment went from Boston to Seattle. Looking at the distance table, we can see that this shipment should normally take seven days. However, the shipment left on September 15th and arrived on January 23rd. The total shipment time is eight days, therefore we can then calculate the days overdue as eight to seven, or one day.

3. Footer

The total late shipments is simply a count of the number of line items in the report. Management finds this type of summary information to be useful when quickly glancing at a report.

As we work through the syntax of SQL, we will return to this report and write an actual SQL query to produce the desired results.

1.11.1 ON YOUR OWN EXERCISE

Management would like a report of all shipments from Boston to London, the captain, the shipment date, the arrival date, the number of days and the total weight for the shipment. The reporting period will be entered by the user. A sample report is shown in Figure 1.13.

The best approach to determining the data elements needed is to complete a table similar to Table 1.1. We have created a similar table for you to complete:

In order to help you to understand the data a little better, please answer the following questions:

5.1 How would you obtain the captain's name?

5.2 How would you calculate the number of days for the shipment to arrive?

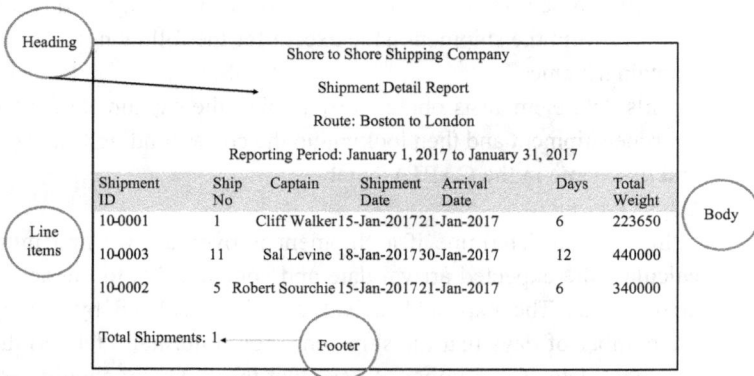

Figure 1.13. Sample report.

Table 1.1. Data elements

Data element	Table	Column
Shipment ID		
Ship no		
Captain		
Shipment date		
Arrival date		
Days		
Total weight	Shipment_Line Item	Calculated

5.3 Now, let's look at the total weight element. When you first examine the report request, you might think that total weight can be determined from the shipment table. However, we do not store the total weight. Looking at the item table, we see that there is a weight for each item. Now, let's look at the shipment_line table. Notice that there is a quantity for each item that is shipped in a shipment. We can calculate the total weight for one item in a shipment by multiplying the weight of the item by the number of items (quantity). However, this only gives us a part of the picture. Since a shipment is made up of many items, how do we calculate the total weight for the shipment?

1.12 SUMMARY

In this chapter, we looked at the Shore to Shore Shipping case study with an eye for thinking like the query engine of a relational database management system (RDBMS) when trying to find data from the tables.

CHAPTER 2

BASIC SQL SYNTAX

In this chapter, we will introduce SQL syntax and some basic SQL commands. The examples used in this section are taken from the Shore-to-Shore Shipping case study introduced in Chapter 1.

2.1 OBJECTIVES

- Discuss basic SQL syntax.
- Discuss thinking through queries.
- Discuss problem solving using relational databases.

2.2 SYNTAX OF AN SQL STATEMENT

SQL statements consist of English-like commands. There are several different SQL commands, each of which performs a specific task. We will focus most of our discussion upon the Select statement, which is used for querying databases. As we progress through the text, we will introduce each component of the select statement. Unlike many programming languages, select statements are not case sensitive.

In its simplest form, the Select statement contains two lines specifying the output of the query as well as the table from which to take the output. The syntax is as follows:

Select $\{expr_1\}, \{expr_2\}, ..., \{expr_n\}$ffrom $\{table\}$;

The expression list can consist of field names, functions, user-defined functions, and mathematical formulas. When we use a field name, we may want to include the name of the table as well as the field name. This is called dot notation.

Let's look at a few examples.

1.1 List the last name of all captains.

```
select lname
from captain;
```

The results of this query are listed in Figure 2.1.
This query could have been written using dot notation as follows:

```
select captain.lname
from captain;
```

Dot notation is not as important to us right now, however it will become more important once we begin to query more than one table in a single select statement.

1.2 List the manufacturer_ID, name and city of all manufacturers.

```
select manufacturer_id, name, city
from manufacturer;
```

The results of this query are listed in Figure 2.2.

Sourchie
Walker
Smith
Levine
Moore
Westmoreland
Gray
Vollage
Nesmith
Levinchuck
Smith
Rice

Figure 2.1. Results of all captains query.

manufacturer_id	name	city
210	United Ship Builders	Bath
211	General Ship Builders	San Diego
212	Master Dynamics	Bridgeport
213	Asia West Ship Builders	Hong Kong
214	Pacific Ship Builders	Fairbanks
215	Best Industries	Seattle
216	Union Corp	Buffalo

Figure 2.2. Manufacturer query results.

2.2.1 ON YOUR OWN EXERCISES

Try writing the following queries.
1.1 List the shipment_id, destination and origin of each shipment.
1.2 List the item number and description of each item.

2.3 EXPRESSIONS IN THE SELECT CLAUSE

Let's start to roll our sleeves up and get into the inner workings of SQL. Let's review the syntax of an SQL statement:

Select *{expr₁}, {expr₂}, ..., {exprₙ}*
from *{table}*;

Recall from our previous discussion that *expr* could be a field (such as lname), a function, a user-defined function or a mathematical formula. We have already shown you some queries using fields. Now, let's look at a few functions that can be used as part of a select. These functions can be used in several ways, including operations on groups. At this point in our discussion, we will only consider how to use these functions to return a single number that acts upon an entire set of records.

2.3.1 MAX AND MIN

The Max function returns the maximum value in our result set based upon the conditions specified in the query. Similarly, the Min function returns the minimum value. Both functions can only be used on numeric datatypes. For example, if we wish to find the ship that can carry the most weight, we can write a query on ship and specify the max(capacity) as our expression. Figure 2.3 shows the query and the result returned.

While we can use the min and max function with other fields in the select expression, the results will not be accurate. Figure 2.4 shows an example of using ship_no with max(capacity). The maximum capacity for all ships is displayed yet the first ship_no is also displayed. In MySQL this will work. In other database management systems this will generate an error message. Later on, we will learn about the group by function that will allow us to use functions such as min and max with other fields.

It is perfectly fine to use more than one aggregate function together, such as:

Select min(capacity), max(capacity)
from ship

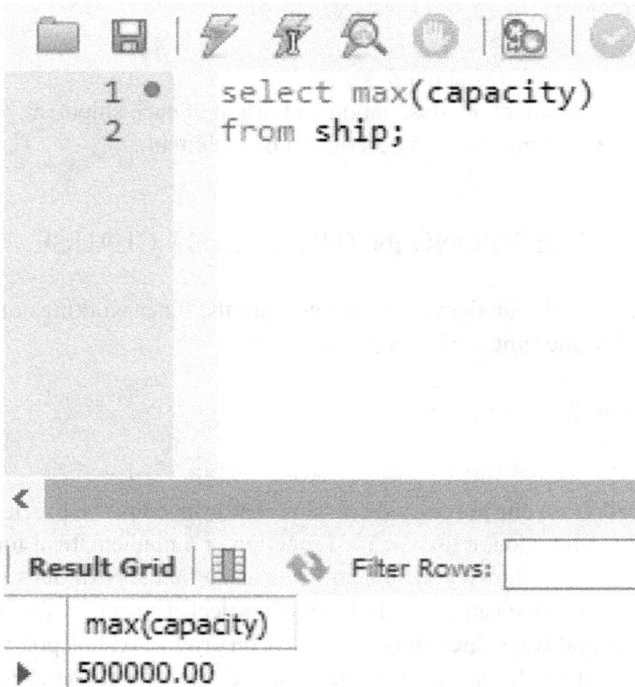

Figure 2.3. Query and results: Ship that can carry the most weight.

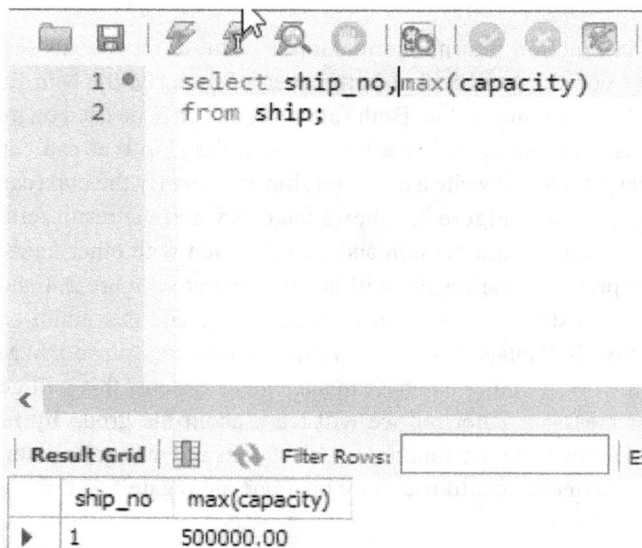

Figure 2.4. Max capacity for ship query.

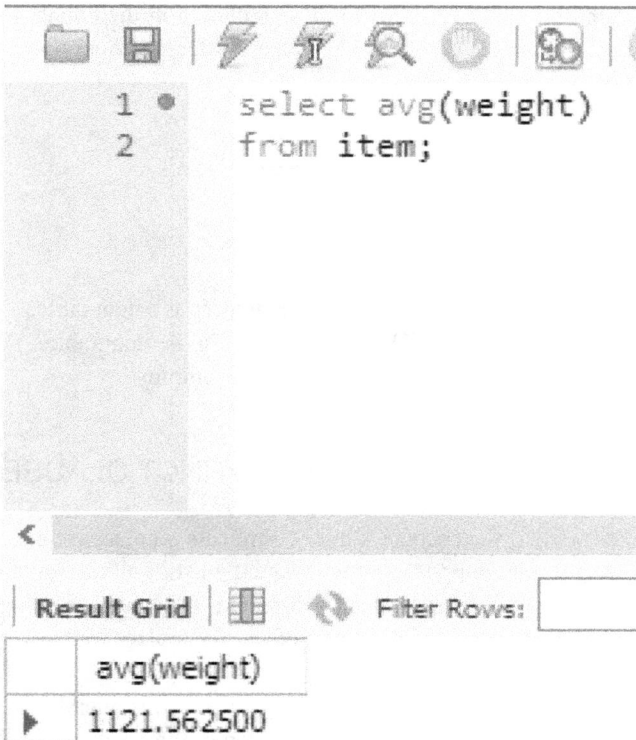

```
1 •     select avg(weight)
2       from item;
```

avg(weight)
▶ 1121.562500

Figure 2.5. Average weight of all items query and results.

2.3.2 AVG

The AVG function computes the average of a numeric field in the result set. Figure 2.5 illustrates a query computing the average weight of all items.

2.3.3 COUNT

The count function returns the number of rows, or records, returned by a query. It takes as a parameter either the name of a field or an asterisk (*). Using the asterisk will result in all rows being returned. For example, if we would like to count the number of shipments, we would type:

select count(*) from shipment;

If we include a field name, such as ship_no, the count function will return the number of rows that contain data for ship_no. If ship_no is empty for some reason, that record will not be included in the count. This will become more important to consider once we look at querying multiple tables using a join command.

2.3.4 ON YOUR OWN EXERCISES

Write queries to answer the following questions:

2.1. What is the weight of the heaviest item in the item table.
2.2. What is the weight of the lightest item in the item table.
2.3. How many captains does the company employ?

2.4 EXTENDING SQL: THE DISTINCT CLAUSE

Often times, when we execute a query duplicate data are returned. Let's look at an example. Suppose that we wanted a list of all the captains who had been the captain of at least one shipment. Of course, we might first think about how to get this information from the tables. We know that the capt_id is in the shipment table. We could then write a query to produce the list of captains. Figure 2.6 shows the results of this query.

You will notice upon careful examination of the result set that several captains are the captains of more than one shipment. This results in two entries for each of these captains. There is a keyword that we can include in our select statement, *distinct*, that will eliminate any duplicate rows in the result set.

Figure 2.7 shows the result of using the distinct clause.

Distinct can also be included in queries that return more than one field. The distinct keyword will act upon the entire row; return only rows that have a unique combination of fields. For example, in Figure 2.8a we show a query of Origin and Destination pairs from the shipment table. Notice that there are several duplicate rows returned in the result set. For example, we have two Boston to Seattle trips, two Seattle to London and three Boston to London trips, and so on. Figure 2.8b shows the use of the distinct clause. Notice that we now have only one record returned for Boston to Seattle, Boston to London, and Seattle to London.

The distinct clause can also be used in the *count* function with a field name.

When would you use the distinct clause with the count? Consider our example in Figure 2.9. If management wanted a report to see whether they were utilizing their pool of captains to the fullest potential, they would not

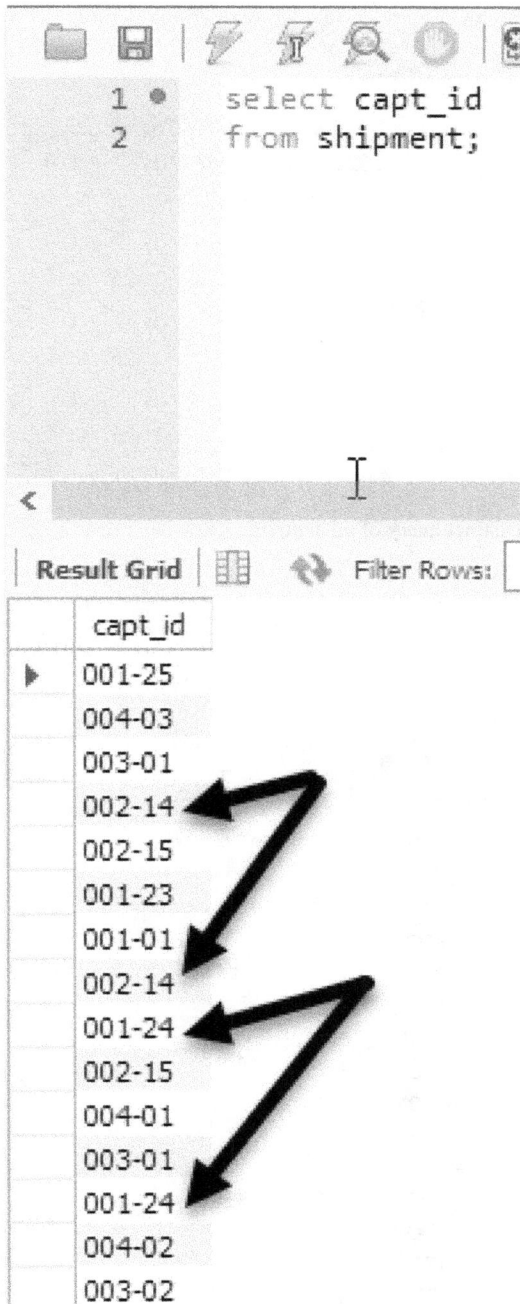

Figure 2.6. Query of all captains.

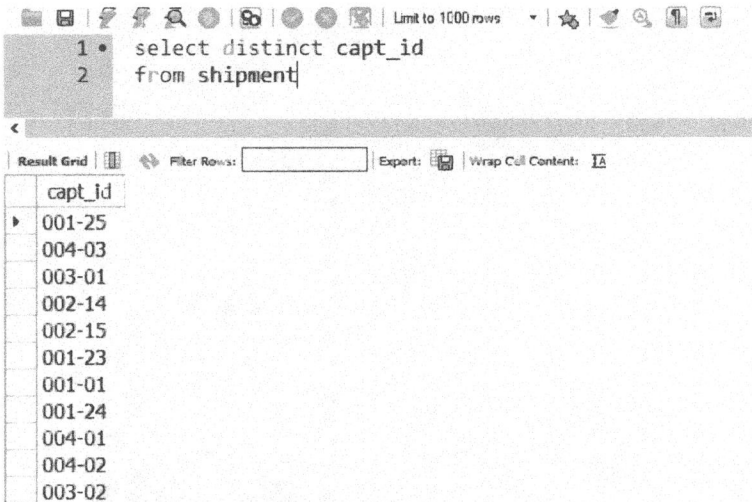

Figure 2.7. Distinct query of all captains.

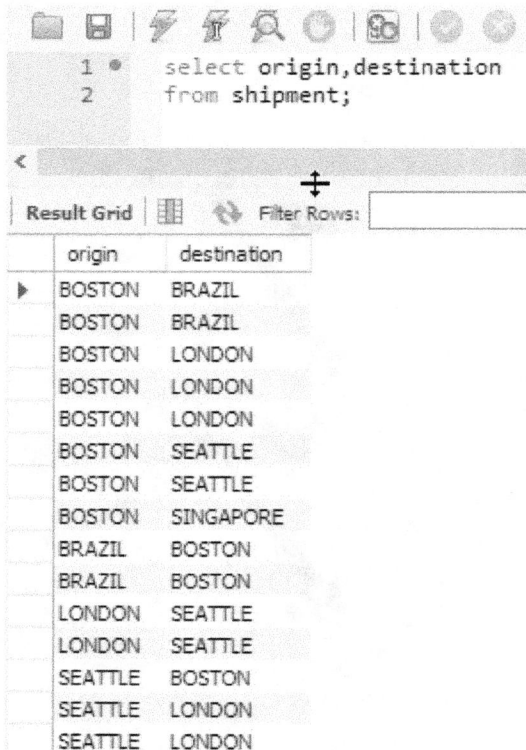

Figure 2.8a. Origin and destination pairs query and results.

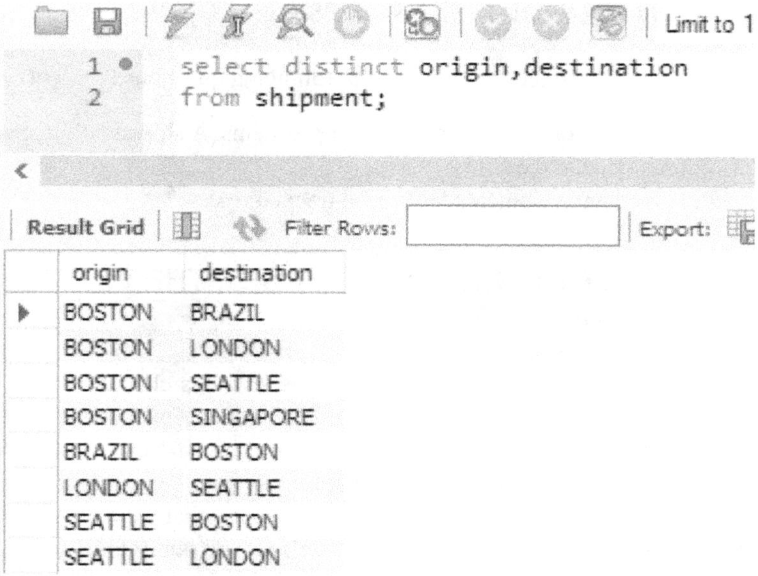

Figure 2.8b. Distinct origin and destination pairs query and results.

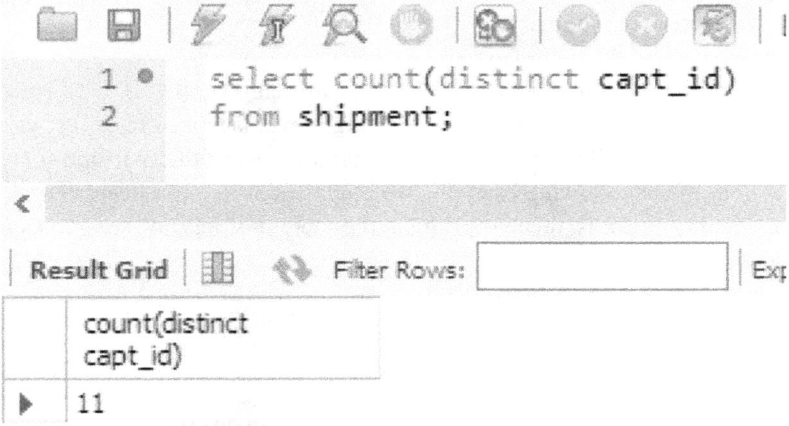

Figure 2.9. Count distinct query.

want to know how many shipments went out with a captain. We already know that each shipment has one captain. However, if there were 10 shipments and 2 shipments had the same captain, all that we would care about in such a report would be the distinct (nonduplicate) number of captains. Figure 2.9 shows such a query and the results.

2.4.1   ON YOUR OWN EXERCISES:

Write and execute queries to answer the following questions:

3.1. List all of the ships that have shipped items. A ship should appear only once in the list.
3.2. How many shipments have been tracked to date?

2.5   QUALIFYING THE RESULT SET: THE WHERE CLAUSE

As you worked through some of the exercises in this chapter, you may have begun to think about ways to qualify the data. For example, what if management wanted to see a list of the capt_ids of captains only for shipments that left from Boston? Another request which you might expect would be to show a report for a period time. From what we have seen so far, there is no way to do this. However, let's extend our definition of the basic SQL clause to include a *where* clause:

Select *{expr₁}, {expr₂}, ..., {exprₙ}*
from *{table}*
where *{condition}*;

You could think of the *where* clause as being similar to an *if* statement in a programming language. In a high-level language like C++, you might test to see if a particular variable has a value and then perform some action. In our following example, we might test to see if a license_grade is equal to 1. If it is, then we print out the capt_id. If it is not, we move on to the next statement.

If (license_grade == 1)
cout<<capt_id;

In a similar way, the *where* clause acts upon a table. In order to list out the capt_ids of captains with a license_grade of 1, we would add a where clause to our select statement. Figure 2.10 shows the results of this query.

Let's try a few other queries. Suppose that we want to find the item number for all of the items with a weight greater than 500. The best approach to composing a query is to think about what you want for output. We need the item_no from the item table. Therefore, our select statement would start out as follows:

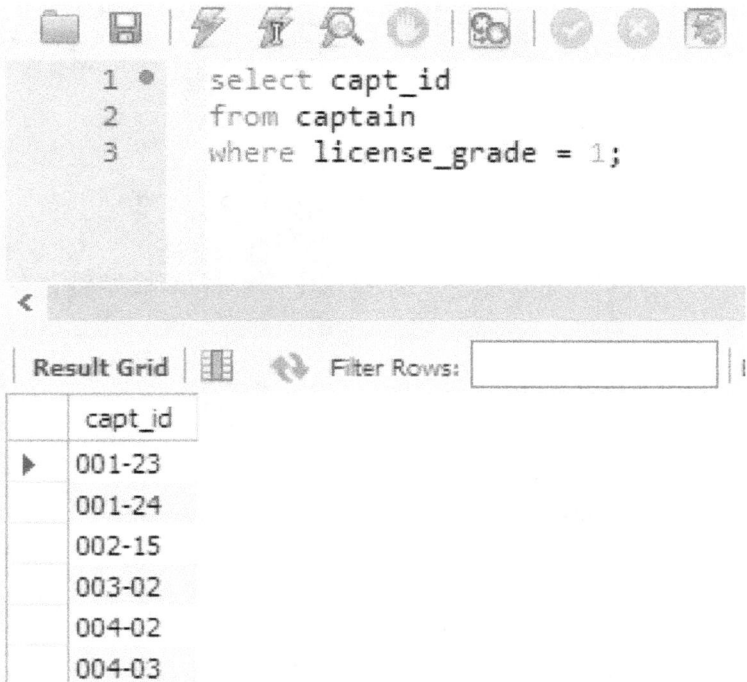

```
1 •    select capt_id
2      from captain
3      where license_grade = 1;
```

	capt_id
▶	001-23
	001-24
	002-15
	003-02
	004-02
	004-03

Figure 2.10. Captains with license_grade of 1 query and results.

Select item_no
from item

If we ran just this query, we would get back a list of all item numbers. However, we want to find only items weighing more than 500 pounds. We can use the greater than (>) relational operator to select only those records that meet our condition. Let's add that to the statement:

Select item_no
from item
where weight > 500;

The results of our query are displayed in Figure 2.11.

Notice that weight does not appear as one of the expressions in the select statement. A member of a condition does not have to be a part of the select statement. This query used the greater than (>) relational operator. SQL, like most programming languages, has many relational operators that can be used in conditions. Table 2.1 presents a list of these operators.

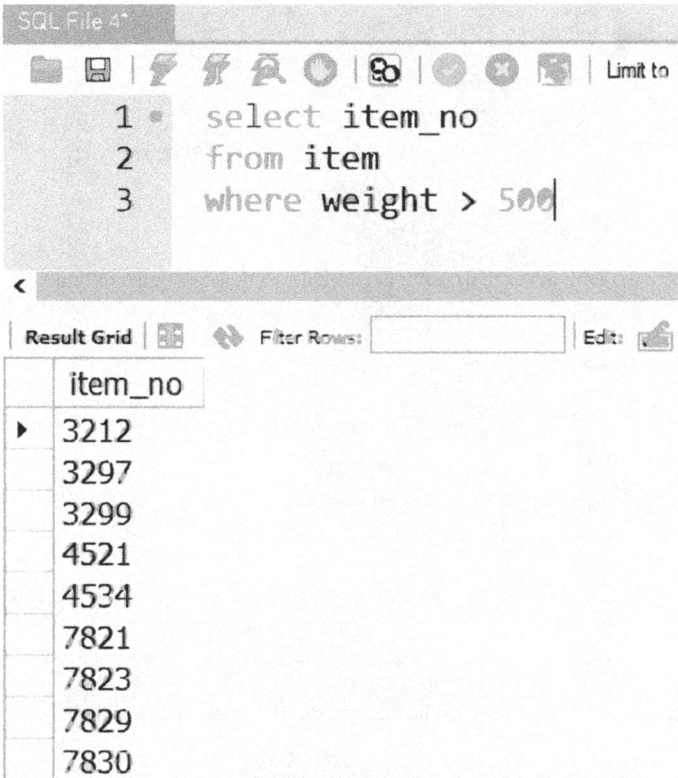

Figure 2.11. Results of query for items with weight > 500.

Table 2.1. Relational operators in SQL

Operator	Meaning
<	Less than
>	Greater than
=	Equal
<=	Less than or equal
>=	Greater than or equal
!=	Not equal
<>	Not equal

2.5.1 ON YOUR OWN EXERCISES

Write queries to answer the following questions:

    4.1. List the ids of all captains with a license_grade of a 1.
    4.2. List the ship numbers of all ships that had captain 001-24 as the captain of at least one shipment.

2.6 PUTTING IT ALL TOGETHER: SELECTIVE AGGREGATION

Learning SQL is like learning a foreign language. Each new construct builds upon others. In this chapter, we have looked at functions, the use of the distinct clause and the where clause. Let's put them together now in a few example queries. When we discussed functions, you were told that a function such as Min, Max, Avg or Count considers the entire result set. However, if we add a where clause to the Select statement, the RDBMS will first process the conditional statement and eliminate any unnecessary rows. Next, the Min, Max, Avg or Count will be computed *based upon the result set after applying the condition.* Consider the following example: Find the maximum weight of all items of type BL. The best way to break down such a query is to first think about what we want to produce for results. We need the maximum weight, so we would start by writing:

    Select max(weight)
    from item

If we executed this query, we would get the maximum weight of all items. However, we want only those items of type 'BL.' We must add the where condition to the query as follows:

    Select max(weight)
    from item
    where item_type = 'BL';

We can modify the query slightly as follows to get the count:

    Select count(*)
    from item
    where item_type = 'BL';

2.7 SUMMARY

In this chapter we have looked at single table queries as well as aggregation. We will next further explore single table queries.

CHAPTER 3

SINGLE TABLE QUERIES

3.1 INTRODUCTION

In this section, we will revisit the where clause and expand upon our discussion by including compound conditions and special operators. We will also learn how to use fields to return a calculated value and discuss sorting result sets.

3.2 OBJECTIVES

- Explain how to write queries to access data from one table
- Describe the use of aggregate functions

3.3 REVIEW

As you recall, we began our discussion of the where clause in the last chapter. We defined the syntax of an SQL select statement as:

Select *{expr₁},{expr₂}, ...,{exprₙ}*
from *{table}*
where *{condition};*

We also discussed relational operators and how these can be used in the where clause.

Let's briefly review with another example from our Shore to Shore Shipping Company case study.

3.3.1 EXAMPLE 3.1

The management of Shore to Shore would like a list of all items that weigh more than 500 pounds. We will use the where clause with the greater than (>) relational operator to execute the query shown in Figure 3.1.

Now, we will move forward in our discussion and extend the where clause to allow for more advanced queries using relational operators. We will also examine a few special operators that we can use with the where clause to enable us to easily write certain types of conditions.

3.4 LOGICAL OPERATORS

Logical operators are used often in everyday life. For example, you may go to a movie on Saturday night *and* go to your favorite restaurant. Your

```
1 •  select item_no,description
2    from item
3    where weight > 500
```

item_no	description
3212	Cement
3297	Steel Beam
3299	Small Steel Plate
4521	5/8" Plywood - 200 sheets/pallet
4534	3/4" Plywood - 200 sheets/pallet
7821	Toyota Camry
7823	Mercury Sable
7829	Mercedes
7830	Honda Accord

Figure 3.1. Query of all items weighing more than 500 pounds using > operator.

Table 3.1. Sample decision table

Statement	Dinner	Play
go to dinner *and* play	True	True
go to dinner *or* play	True	False
	False	True
not go to dinner *and not* go to play	False	False

significant other may ask you if you would like to go to a movie on Saturday night *or* to a play. In the realm of computer science, we generally deal with three logical operators: *and, or,* and *not.*

In order to understand a little better how these operators work, let's organize our choices for what to do on Saturday evening into a table (see Table 3.1).

Notice that the *and* operator only applies when both dinner and play are true. The *or* operator only is valid when either dinner is true or when play is true. The *not* operator only is applicable when a value is false. In the third example in the table, we combine the *not* with the *and* to express the fact that both conditions are false.

3.4.1 EXAMPLE 3.2

The management of Shore to Shore would like to list out all items that are of type "BL" (building materials) *and* weigh more than 500 pounds. We would write the where clause of this query using the *and* logical operator along with the greater than (>) relational operator.

3.5 ON YOUR OWN EXERCISES

In order to make sure that you understand how logical operators work, fill out Table 3.2 with the left side, relational operator and right side of the where clauses needed to answer each query. We have provided the answer to the first three queries. Do not be concerned with the specifics of the select clause, just focus on the where clause.

3.6 COMPOUND WHERE CLAUSES

Now that we have explained logical operators, let's look at how we can apply these directly to queries through the use of compound where

Table 3.2. Table for on-your-own exercises

Query	First condition	Logical operator(s)	Second condition
Find all class one ships manufactured by manufacturer_id 211	ship.class = 1	And	ship.manufacturer_id = 211
Find all ships that have a capacity > 100,000 pounds or are class 2	ship.capacity> 100,000	Or	ship.class = 2
Find all ships that have a capacity > 50,000 pounds and are not class 2	ship.capacity> 50,000	and not	ship.class = 3
Find all ships that are class 1 and have a capacity <500,000 pounds			
Find all items that are of type FP and weigh less than 200 pounds			
Find all items that are of type FP and weight less than 200 pounds (use the > relational operator and the not logical operator)			
Find all shipments that originated in Boston or in London			
Find all origin/ destination pairs that take no more than 5 days and have a distance of 5,000 miles or more			

clauses. You have had the opportunity to write a few sample compound where clauses in the previous on-your-own exercises. Now, let's look at a few examples.

3.6.1 EXAMPLE 3.3

In example 3.1, we produced a list of items that weighed more than 500 pounds. Now, management has asked us to produce a list of all wood products weighing more than 500 pounds. In order to solve this problem, we need to find all items that have a type of "WP" *and* have a weight of more than 500 pounds. The query is shown in Figure 3.2.

3.6.2 EXAMPLE 3.4

Management would like a list of all items that are either a food product or a building material. In order to solve this, we need to write a query which displays all items with a type "FP" *or* a type of "BL." The query is shown in Figure 3.3.

3.6.3 EXAMPLE 3.5

Another query that might prove useful is to find all items that weigh more than 2,000 pounds and are not building materials. In order to create this query, we would use the *and* as well as the *not* logical operators. The query is shown in Figure 3.4.

```
1 • select item_no,description
2   from item
3   where weight > 500
4   and item_type = 'WP'
```

item_no	description
4521	5/8" Plywood - 200 sheets/pallet
4534	3/4" Plywood - 200 sheets/pallet

Figure 3.2. Query of all items of type WP and weight > 500.

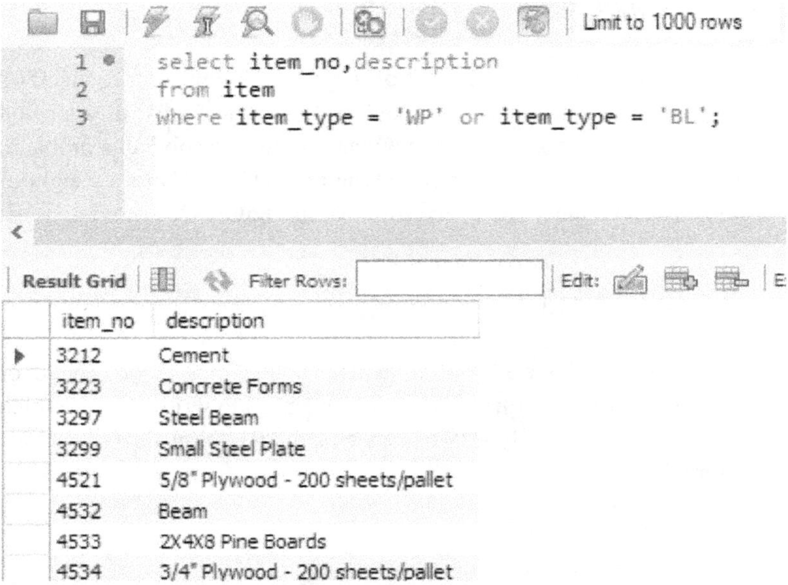

Figure 3.3. Query of all items of type WP or BL.

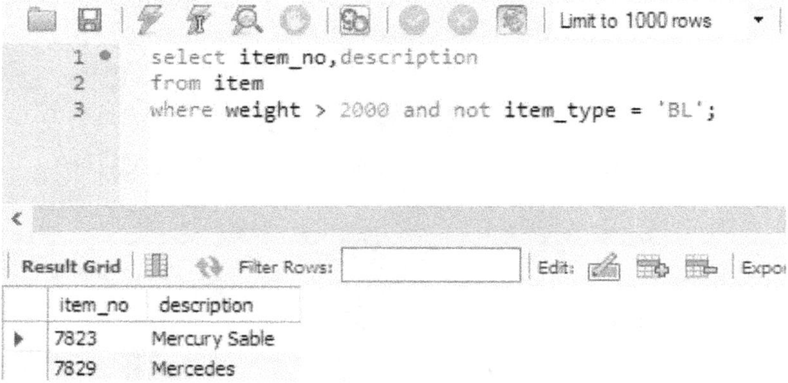

Figure 3.4. Query of all items that weight more than 2,000 pounds and are not building materials.

Many times in SQL, there is more than one way of performing a query. Instead of using the *not* logical operator, we could also have used the != relational operator. The same query using the != operator is shown in Figure 3.5.

Figure 3.5. Query from Figure 3.4 with != operator.

3.6.4 ON YOUR OWN EXERCISES

1.1 Find all items that are of type "WP" and weigh less than 500 pounds.
1.2 Find all ships that are not class 1 and have a capacity of 50,000 pounds or more.
1.3 Find all shipments that originate in Boston or Seattle.

3.7 ORDER OF OPERATOR PRECEDENCE

In mathematics, we evaluate operators in a certain order. For example, given the following equation:

$$a = b * c + d/e$$

where $b = 2$, $c = 3$, $d = 4$ and $e = 2$.

First, you would perform the multiplication, then the division and then the addition as follows:

$$a = 2*3 + 4/2$$
$$a = 6 + 2$$
$$a = 8$$

This result is dramatically different if we don't follow rules of operator precedence and just work from left to right:

$$a = 2*3 + 4/2$$
$$a = 6 + 4/2$$

$$a = 10/2$$
$$a = 5$$

From very early on in your math training, you were taught two rules: associativity and operator precedence. Associativity tells us to evaluate expressions from the left to the right. Operator precedence tells us which types of operators to evaluate before others. In our previous example, we followed rules of precedence that tell us to evaluate the multiplication (*) and division (/) operators before the addition (+) and subtraction (-) operators. These rules can be broken through the use of parenthesis. For example, $a = b * (c+d)/e$ would tell us to evaluate the c+d first and then the rest of the expressions.

All of the rules that we have learned from math can be applied to SQL. We will look in a bit more detail at computed columns and see how we can use these rules.

The logical operators also have rules of precedence. The *and* operator takes precedence over the *or*. The *not* operator has a higher precedence over the *and* and the *or*. For example, if we have the following expressions:

A evaluates to true
B evaluates to false
C evaluates to false
D = A or B and C would evaluate as follows
    D = true or true and false
    D = true or false
    D = true

If we did not follow an order of precedence, we would get different results:

    D = true or true and false
    D = true and false
    D = false

Let's look at a few more examples.

3.7.1 EXAMPLE 3.6

Management would like a report that will show all shipments that originated in Seattle or Boston. For those shipments that originated in Boston,

```
1 •   select shipment_id, capt_id,ship_no,shipment_date,origin
2     from shipment
3     where origin = 'SEATTLE' or origin = 'BOSTON' and capt_id = '001-24';
```

shipment_id	capt_id	ship_no	shipment_date	origin
09-0001	001-25	25	2016-03-12	SEATTLE
10-0002	001-01	5	2017-01-15	SEATTLE
10-0004	001-24	39	2017-03-13	BOSTON
11-0004	001-24	16	2018-09-01	SEATTLE

Figure 3.6. Query of shipments that originated in Boston and had captain 001-24 as captain.

management only wants to see the ones that had captain 001-24 as the captain. Figure 3.6 shows our query and the results.

Notice that the order of precedence dictated that the Boston and capt_id = '001-24' were evaluated first, and then the *or* was evaluated next.

3.7.2   EXAMPLE 3.7

We would like to create a report of all shipments that John Smith (capt_id 001-24) was the captain of and that originated either out of Boston or Seattle. At first, we might be inclined to think that the query in Figure 3.6 would give us the correct results. However, remember that the *and* is evaluated first, so only those shipments that originated in Boston with John Smith as the captain would be included, as well as all shipments that originated in Seattle. In order to change this, we need to cause the query optimizer to evaluate the *or* first. We can do this by placing the expression with the *or* in parenthesis. Figure 3.7 shows this query and the results.

```
1 •   select shipment_id, capt_id,ship_no,shipment_date,origin
2     from shipment
3     where (origin = 'SEATTLE' or origin = 'BOSTON') and capt_id = '001-24';
```

shipment_id	capt_id	ship_no	shipment_date	origin
10-0004	001-24	39	2017-03-13	BOSTON
11-0004	001-24	16	2018-09-01	SEATTLE

Figure 3.7. Query of John Smith's shipments from Boston or Seattle.

3.7.3 ON YOUR OWN EXERCISES

2.1 List all building materials and wood products that weigh less than 500 pounds.
2.2 List all building materials and only wood products that weigh more than 500 pounds.
2.3 List all class 1 ships with a capacity greater than or equal to 250,000 pounds and all class 1 ships manufactured by manufacturer_id 212.

3.8 SPECIAL OPERATORS

There are several special operators that we use in the where clause. We will discuss each one in depth with some examples.

3.8.1 BETWEEN

The between operator is used when your comparison condition might include an upper and lower range. For example, if you would like to find all ships that have a capacity between 50,000 and 100,000 pounds, you could use the between operator or you could use a compound where condition. Figure 3.8a shows the use of the between operator and Figure 3.8b shows a compound conditional using the *and* operator. Both are equivalent.

Let's look at another example. Management would like a report of all items that weigh more than 500 pounds and less than 1,000 pounds. Again, we could use the between operator. Figure 3.9 shows the query and the result.

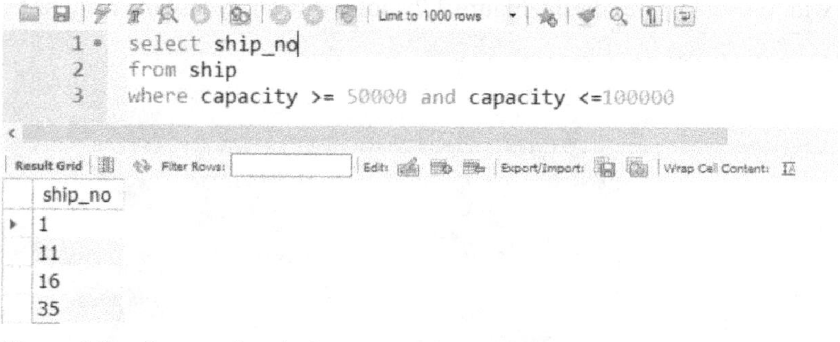

Figure 3.8a. Query using the between operator.

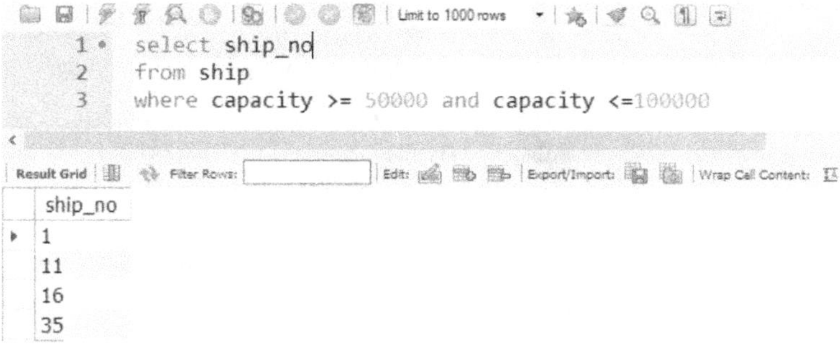
Limit to 1000 rows
1 select ship_no
2 from ship
3 where capacity >= 50000 and capacity <=100000
Result Grid
Filter Rows:
Edit:
Export/Import:
Wrap Cell Content:
ship_no
1
11
16
35

Figure 3.8b. Query using a compound conditional.

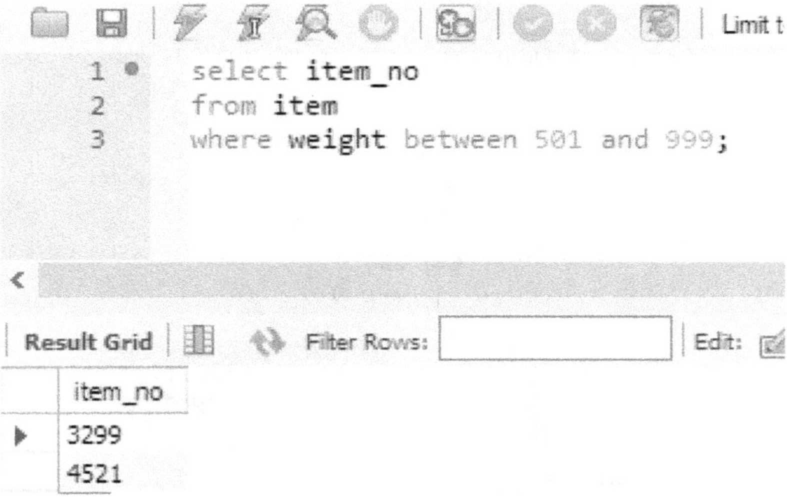
Limit t
1 select item_no
2 from item
3 where weight between 501 and 999;
Result Grid
Filter Rows:
Edit:
item_no
3299
4521

Figure 3.9. Query of all items weighing more than 500 pounds using between operator.

3.8.2 LIKE

There are sometimes cases where you may need to query based upon only a portion of the information that is contained in a particular field. Most relational database management systems provide us with the capability to do this through the use of the Like operator with wildcard characters. The wildcard characters in SQL are the % symbols. For example, if we wanted to find all captains whose last name began with S, we would place the % after the S. If we wanted to find all captains whose last name ended with an e, we would place the % before the e. Figure 3.10a and Figure 3.10b show these two queries.

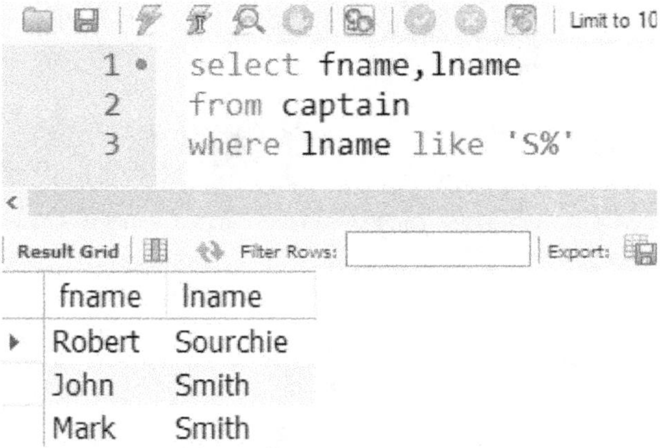

```
1 •   select fname,lname
2     from captain
3     where lname like 'S%'
```

fname	lname
▶ Robert	Sourchie
John	Smith
Mark	Smith

Figure 3.10a. Query of all captains whose last name begins with an s.

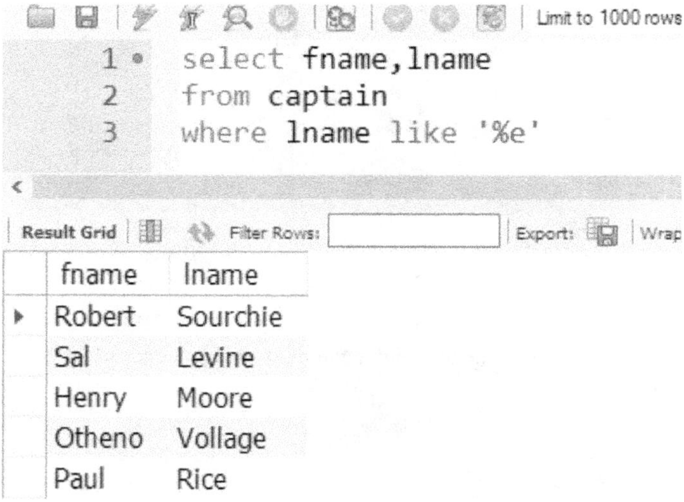

```
1 •   select fname,lname
2     from captain
3     where lname like '%e'
```

fname	lname
▶ Robert	Sourchie
Sal	Levine
Henry	Moore
Otheno	Vollage
Paul	Rice

Figure 3.10b. Query of all captains whose last name ends with e using wildcard.

The wildcard character can also be used both in front of and behind a letter to find all occurrences of a field that contains that letter. For example, if we would like to find all captains whose last name contains an e in any position, we would write the query shown in Figure 3.11.

Please keep in mind that the letter that we are searching for is case sensitive.

```
1 •  select fname,lname
2    from captain
3    where lname like '%e%'
```

fname	lname
Robert	Sourchie
Cliff	Walker
Sal	Levine
Henry	Moore
James	Westmoreland
Otheno	Vollage
Marcia	Nesmith
Paul	Rice
Phillip	Levinchuck

Figure 3.11. Query of all captains whose last name contains an e.

3.8.3 IN

Previously, we showed many uses for the *or* logical operator. As we had discussed, logical operators can be put together to form a series of conditions. However, this can at times be tedious to write. For example, if you wanted to find all the shipment ids for shipments that contained item 4532 or item 7823 or item 2101 or item 2123, you could write the query using several *or* italics as shown in Figure 3.12a or you could use the In statement, as shown in Figure 3.12b.

We will also see the in operator used later on for subqueries.

3.9 COMPUTED COLUMNS

We've looked at using special functions in our select statements to count the number of rows that meet a certain condition or to add together numbers. There are also times when we may want to perform a calculation on a column. One example of this might be to convert the weight of each item from pounds to kilograms. This can be done by performing the computation right in the select statement, as follows:

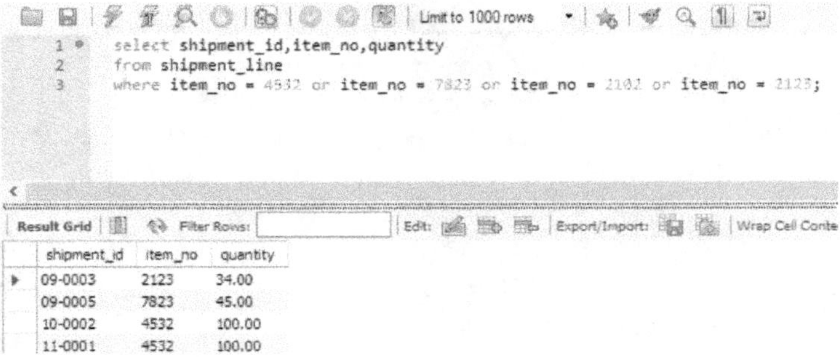

Figure 3.12a. Example query using or operator.

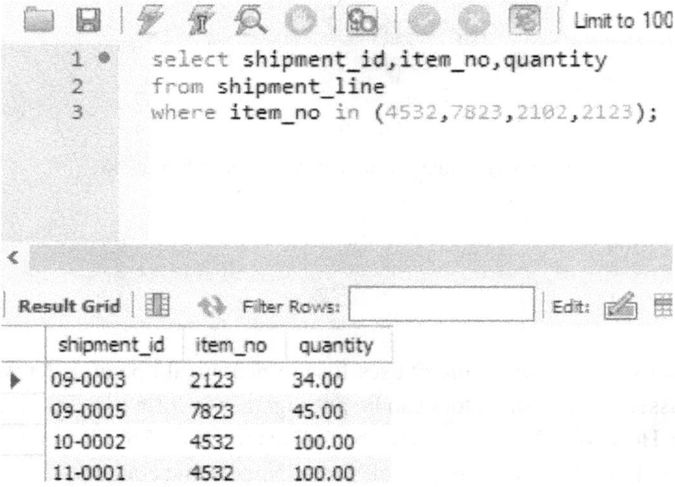

Figure 3.12b. Example query using in statement.

```
select item_no, weight, weight*.4536
from item;
```

If we were to run this, we would notice that the computed column would have a title that is not very descriptive. We also would not be able to reference this column as easily in a where clause later on in the select. In order to make things a bit clearer, we could include an alias to the computed column. The alias is specified by using the as clause as follows:

```
select item_no, weight, weight*.4536 as kiloweight
from item;
```

Each time you run this query now, the computed weight is displayed as kiloweight and we can reference the computed column as kiloweight.

3.10   THE ORDER BY CLAUSE

The order by clause is used to sort the results of your query. We can specify one column in the select statement or many columns, all separated by commas. Computed columns can also be included in the order by clause. The order by clause is not required, but can be added to any query. For example, if we would like to sort the captain table by last name, we would run the table shown in Figure 3.13.

You can also include the *desc* keyword to sort in descending order (Z to A). Figure 3.14 is an example of this.

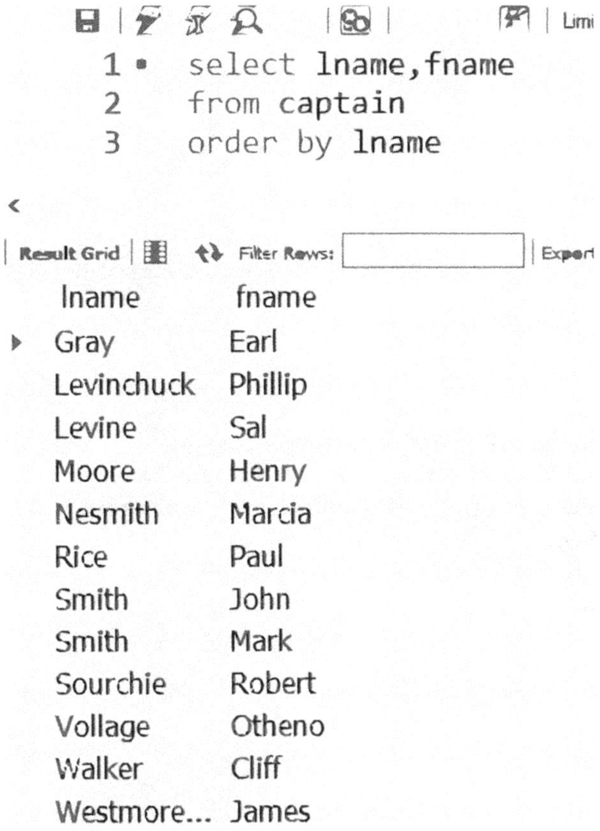

Figure 3.13. Query to sort captain table by last name.

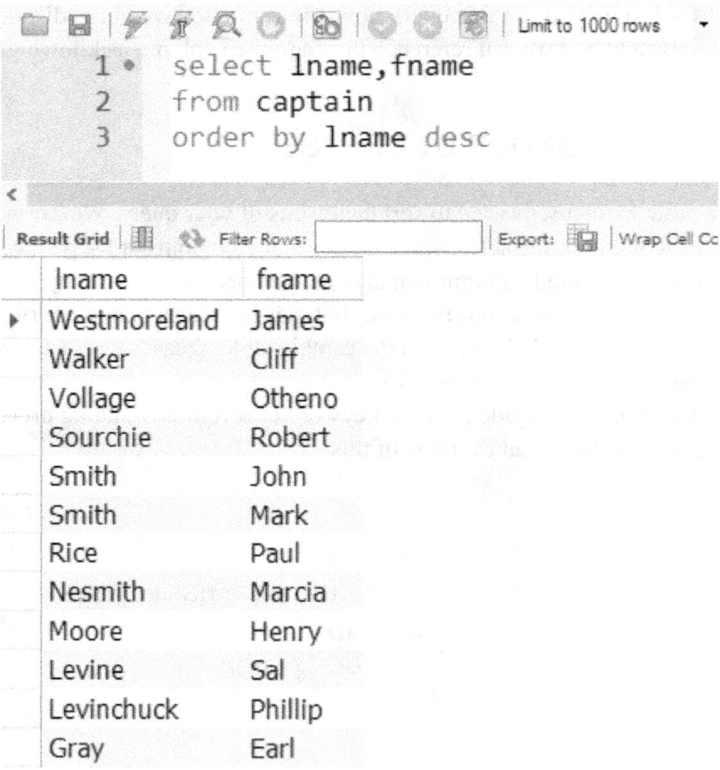

Figure 3.14. Query to sort captain table by last name in descending order.

3.11 SUMMARY

In this chapter we looked at performing queries on single tables. We also looked at using several different operators for aggregation as well as wildcards. All of this will form a good basis as we move along in learning SQL.

CHAPTER 4

INTRODUCTION TO JOINS

4.1 INTRODUCTION

In the last chapter, we looked at how to query a single table. While this is quite useful, many times we will need to join more than one table in order to get the results that we want. In this chapter we will begin to look at join operations and finish up with our discussion in Chapter 5.

4.2 OBJECTIVES

- Introduce multiple-table queries.
- Discuss basic joins

4.3 MULTIPLE-TABLE QUERIES

When the Shore to Shore Shipping Company case study was introduced in Chapter 1, we looked at several examples where you had to examine information from more than one table. The objective in writing down some of these queries was to begin to think in SQL. However, our discussion of SQL up to this point has only covered single table queries. As we have seen in our examples, there are many cases where we would like to look up information in other tables simply for display purposes or to select records as part of the conditions of a where clause. There are two basic ways to do this: joins and subqueries. While subqueries can be used to perform all of your join operations, I do not recommend this method for joining more than two tables. However, there are cases where subqueries can only be used and a join would not produce the desired results.

4.4 REFERENTIAL INTEGRITY CONSTRAINTS

Referential integrity constraints tell us how tables are related to one another. Every table has a unique identifier, which can be made up of one or more fields from the table. There can only be one unique identifier for each row of the table. Let's look at the ship table in Figure 4.1

As you can see there is only one ship number 1, one ship 11 and so on. We do have tables in our case study which use more than one field to uniquely identify a row. Let's look at the shipment_line table as shown in Table 4.1.

ship_no	class	capacity	purch_date	manufacturer_id
1	1	100000.00	1965-01-25	212
10	3	20000.00	1976-03-15	210
11	2	50000.00	1971-01-30	210
16	2	75000.00	1975-11-01	215
25	3	15000.00	1979-11-02	213
35	2	55000.00	1989-12-01	211
37	1	250000.00	1990-12-02	216
39	1	500000.00	1991-12-03	211
5	1	120000.00	1969-01-20	212
6	1	500000.00	1969-03-07	212

Figure 4.1. Ship table.

Table 4.1. Shipment_line table

Shipment_id	Item_no	Quantity
09-0001	3223	100
09-0001	3297	87
09-0001	3299	34
09-0002	3212	100
09-0002	3223	50
09-0003	2101	432
09-0003	2109	1000
09-0003	2123	34
09-0003	2125	200
09-0004	3212	10
09-0004	3223	5

09-0005	3297	42
09-0005	7821	5
09-0005	7823	45
10-0001	7821	10
10-0001	7829	3
10-0001	7830	100
10-0002	4521	100
10-0002	4532	100
10-0002	4533	1000
10-0003	4521	100
10-0003	4534	300
10-0004	2101	1000
10-0004	2109	800
10-0004	2125	56
11-0001	4521	10
11-0001	4532	100
11-0002	4533	100
11-0002	4534	15
11-0003	7829	1000
11-0004	3223	150
11-0004	3297	10
11-0005	2101	100
11-0005	2109	1000
11-0006	2125	345
11-0006	7830	30

As you can see, there are multiple rows with the same shipment_id, for example 10-0004. Also, there are multiple rows with the same item_no, for example 4521. However, there is only one row with a combination of shipment_id and item_no. This is called a *composite key*. For example, there is only one row with 10-0004 for the shipment_id and 2125 for the item_no. The unique identifier for a table is called the *primary key*.

While the primary key is a critical part of referential integrity, we also need some mechanism to insure that a reference to another table is accurate. Let's take another look at the ship table as shown in Figure 4.1.

Notice that there is a manufacturer_id in the ship table. When we add a new record to the ship table, we want to be sure that there is a corresponding manufacturer_id. For example, we would not want to add manufacturer_id 301 if no such manufacturer exists. This is called a foreign key constraint. So manufacturer_id is a foreign key in the ship table, referencing manufacturer. Referential integrity constraints will come into play as we next look at joining multiple tables together. Without such integrity, we would have no way of guaranteeing that we could join two tables together. The foreign keys form the basis for join operations.

4.5   JOINING TABLES

Let's first look at an example from our case study. Let's suppose that we want to display the captain's first name and last name for all shipments that originated from Boston. We would first want to look to the shipment table, find all shipments that originated in Boston. Next, we would look up the captain_ids for each shipment and then find the corresponding names. Perhaps our first attempt at writing this in SQL might be something like Query 4.1:

```
select fname,lname,shipment_id,origin
from captain,shipment
where shipment.origin= 'BOSTON';
```

This query will produce the following results shown in Table 4.2.

What happened here? It seems that each row of the captain table was matched with each row of the shipment table. We end up with 96 rows returned. This is called a Cartesian product. While it is not dangerous to do this with a small dataset such as our case study, running a Cartesian product on two large tables could take up significant resources on your database server. The reason that every row of captain is matched with every row of shipment is because the RDBMS does not know how to eliminate records that do not match. Even though a foreign key might be included in the shipment table referencing the captain table, the RDBMS does not automatically use this constraint in order to join the tables. We must *explicitly* define the join condition. In order to join the tables correctly, we need to identify columns in each table that are common. As we discussed earlier, each table has a primary key which uniquely identifies each record in the table. The primary key for Captain is capt_id. The primary key for Shipment is shipment_id. Notice that capt_id also appears in the Shipment table. This is called a foreign key. So, we can join the tables using the capt_id as the common field. The SQL statement to do this is shown in Figure 4.2.

Table 4.2. Results of query 4.1

FNAME	LNAME	SHIPMENT_ID	ORIGIN
Robert	Sourchie	09-0002	BOSTON
Cliff	Walker	09-0002	BOSTON
John	Smith	09-0002	BOSTON
Sal	Levine	09-0002	BOSTON
Henry	Moore	09-0002	BOSTON
James	Westmoreland	09-0002	BOSTON
Earl	Gray	09-0002	BOSTON
Otheno	Vollage	09-0002	BOSTON
Marcia	Nesmith	09-0002	BOSTON
Phillip	Levinchuck	09-0002	BOSTON
Mark	Smith	09-0002	BOSTON
Paul	Rice	09-0002	BOSTON
Robert	Sourchie	09-0005	BOSTON
Cliff	Walker	09-0005	BOSTON
John	Smith	09-0005	BOSTON
Sal	Levine	09-0005	BOSTON
Henry	Moore	09-0005	BOSTON
James	Westmoreland	09-0005	BOSTON
Earl	Gray	09-0005	BOSTON
Otheno	Vollage	09-0005	BOSTON
Marcia	Nesmith	09-0005	BOSTON
Phillip	Levinchuck	09-0005	BOSTON
Mark	Smith	09-0005	BOSTON
Paul	Rice	09-0005	BOSTON
Robert	Sourchie	10-0001	BOSTON
Cliff	Walker	10-0001	BOSTON
John	Smith	10-0001	BOSTON
Sal	Levine	10-0001	BOSTON
Henry	Moore	10-0001	BOSTON
James	Westmoreland	10-0001	BOSTON
Earl	Gray	10-0001	BOSTON
Otheno	Vollage	10-0001	BOSTON
Marcia	Nesmith	10-0001	BOSTON

(Continued)

Table 4.2. (Continued)

Phillip	Levinchuck	10-0001	BOSTON
Mark	Smith	10-0001	BOSTON
Paul	Rice	10-0001	BOSTON
Robert	Sourchie	10-0003	BOSTON
Cliff	Walker	10-0003	BOSTON
John	Smith	10-0003	BOSTON
Sal	Levine	10-0003	BOSTON
Henry	Moore	10-0003	BOSTON
James	Westmoreland	10-0003	BOSTON
Earl	Gray	10-0003	BOSTON
Otheno	Vollage	10-0003	BOSTON
Marcia	Nesmith	10-0003	BOSTON
Phillip	Levinchuck	10-0003	BOSTON
Mark	Smith	10-0003	BOSTON
Paul	Rice	10-0003	BOSTON
Robert	Sourchie	10-0004	BOSTON
Cliff	Walker	10-0004	BOSTON
John	Smith	10-0004	BOSTON
Sal	Levine	10-0004	BOSTON
Henry	Moore	10-0004	BOSTON
James	Westmoreland	10-0004	BOSTON
Earl	Gray	10-0004	BOSTON
Otheno	Vollage	10-0004	BOSTON
Marcia	Nesmith	10-0004	BOSTON
Phillip	Levinchuck	10-0004	BOSTON
Mark	Smith	10-0004	BOSTON
Paul	Rice	10-0004	BOSTON

This can also be written as shown in Figure 4.2 using the ANSI 1992 standard. MySQL and Oracle will accept either syntax. Microsoft products only accept the second convention. The non-ANSI syntax, while still widely used, is not recommended by many vendors. Both ways of writing the queries have the same performance. We will use the ANSI-standard syntax throughout this text. Figure 4.3 shows the query as well as the results.

```
use shoretoshore;
select fname,lname,shipment_id,origin
from captain,shipment
where captain.capt_id = shipment.capt_id
and shipment.origin= 'BOSTON';
```

Figure 4.2. Query to join captain and shipment tables.

```
1 •   select fname,lname,shipment_id,origin
2     from captain inner join shipment
3     on captain.capt_id = shipment.capt_id
4     where shipment.origin= 'BOSTON'
5
6
```

Result Grid | Filter Rows: | Export: | Wrap Cell Content:

fname	lname	shipment_id	origin
Henry	Moore	09-0005	BOSTON
Henry	Moore	11-0001	BOSTON
Cliff	Walker	10-0001	BOSTON
Sal	Levine	10-0003	BOSTON
John	Smith	10-0004	BOSTON
James	Westmoreland	11-0003	BOSTON
Marcia	Nesmith	11-0005	BOSTON
Paul	Rice	09-0002	BOSTON

Figure 4.3. Query to join shipment and captain tables using ANSI 1999 standard SQL.

4.5.1 EXAMPLES

Let's take a look at a couple of examples from our introduction to the case study in Chapter 1. So that you may refer back to Chapter 1, I've referenced the same numbering scheme.

1. Which manufacturer built ship number 37? (Example 1.1)
   Here we should join the manufacturer table with the ship table. The ship table has manufacturer_id as a foreign key and manufacturer_

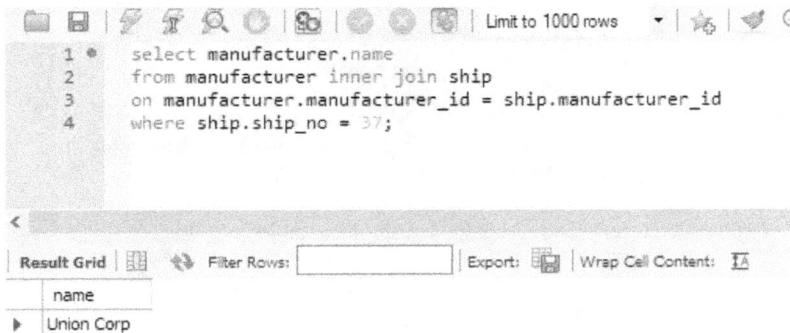

```
1 •   select manufacturer.name
2     from manufacturer inner join ship
3     on manufacturer.manufacturer_id = ship.manufacturer_id
4     where ship.ship_no = 37;
```

Result Grid | Filter Rows: [   ] | Export: | Wrap Cell Content: 🗛

name
▶ Union Corp

Figure 4.4. Query to join manufacturer to ship table to find manufacturer that built ship 37.

id is the primary key in the manufacturer table. The query and result set are shown in Figure 4.4.

A couple of things to make note of here:

- Notice that we include both manufacturer and ship in the from clause, even though we only use manufacturer.name in the select clause.

- We use the full dot notation (manufacturer.name) in the first line of the select clause. In this case, this is optional. It is required if there is more than 1 column with the same name in the referenced tables. For example, if we wanted to list the manufacturer_id, we would need to specify which table this is coming from. If you would like to shorten up the table names when referencing them with the dot notation, you can use an alias, such as m for manufacturer and s for ship. The query with aliases is shown in Query 4.2 as follows:

select m.name
from manufacturer m inner join ship s
on m.manufacturer_id = s.manufacturer_id
where s.ship_no = 37;

2. List the different classes of ships built by manufacturers located in California (Example 1.2).

This query requires a join of two tables and an additional condition in the where clause to select only CA as the state of the manufacturer. The query and result set are shown in Figure 4.5.

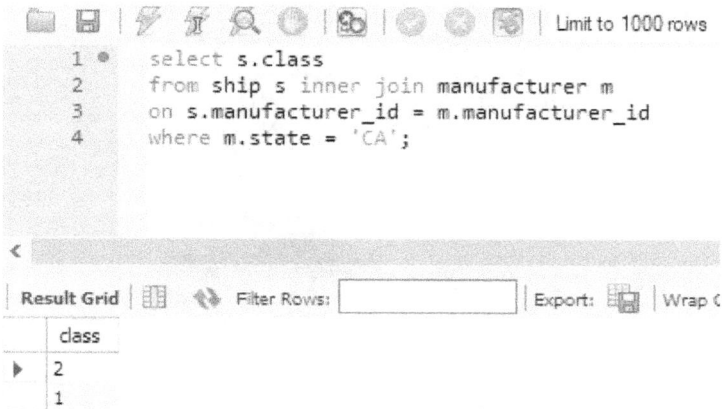

Figure 4.5. Query to find different classes of ships built by manufacturers in California.

4.5.2 ON YOUR OWN EXERCISES

2.1. List the manufacturers of all class 2 ships.

2.2. List the manufacturers of all ships with a capacity of 100,000 pounds or more.

2.3. List all ships purchased after 1975 and manufactured in another country.

4.6 COMPOSITE KEYS

Generally speaking, most join operations require n-1 join conditions, where n is the number of tables. So, a two table join will require 1 join condition, a three table join two, and so on. The only exception to this rule occurs when composite keys are used. The Distance table in our case study is an example of this. Origin and Destination form a composite primary key. In the Shipment table, Origin and Destination form a composite foreign key referencing the Distance table. Let's look at an example:

1. List all shipments that require more than 5 days of travel.
   For this query, we will join the Distance table to the Shipment table using the origin and destination fields. We will also add a condition to select only records for journeys that required more than 5 days of travel. Figure 4.6 shows the query as well as the results.

```
1 •   select shipment.shipment_id
2     from shipment inner join distance
3     on shipment.origin   = distance.origin
4     and shipment.destination = distance.destination
5     where distance.days > 5;
6
7
```

Result Grid | Filter Rows: | Export: | Wrap Cell Content:

shipment_id
11-0003
11-0005
09-0004
11-0006
09-0001
10-0002
11-0004

Figure 4.6. Query to find all shipments that require more than 5 days of travel.

4.7 JOINING MORE THAN TWO TABLES

Many of the problems that you will encounter will require joining multiple tables. In Chapter 1, we introduced a method to think through complex queries. The thought process here is to develop a pathway to get from one place to another. For example, if we wanted to list all of the captains who piloted ships manufactured by a particular manufacturer, we cannot directly link the Captain table to the Manufacturer table. Instead, we would have to go through the Shipment table (since this is the link between Ship and Captain) and the Ship table (since this is the link between Shipment and Manufacturer). As we did in Chapter 1, it is easier to visualize this type of query by making a map. Figure 4.7 shows a map of this query. I've also created a map of the entire case study which you can use for reference for all queries. This can be found at the end of the chapter.

Let's try writing a query. List all captains (last name and first name) who piloted ships manufactured by General Ship Builders. This query as well as the results are shown in Figure 4.8.

Let's look at one additional example: List all shipments that were carried by a ship manufactured by General Ship Builders. The query and results are shown in Figure 4.9.

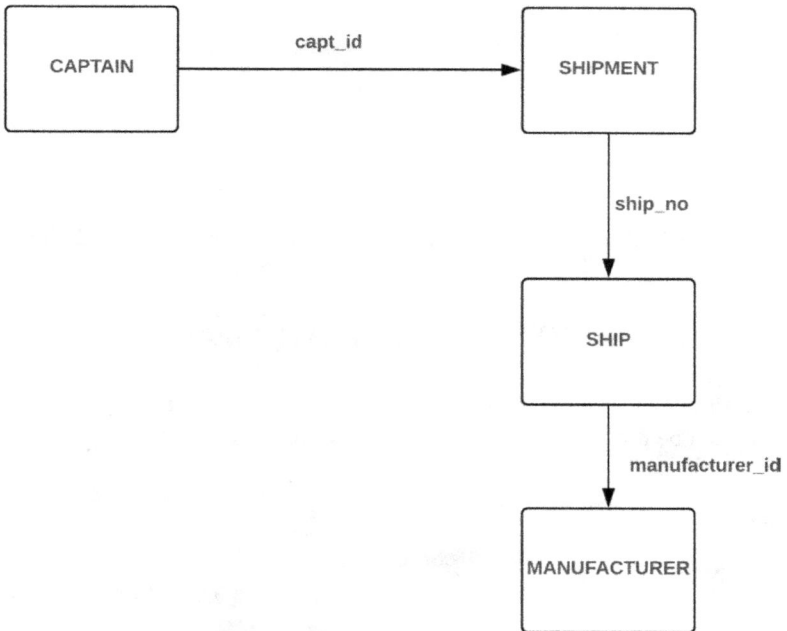

Figure 4.7. Map of query to list captains who piloted ships by certain manufacturers.

Figure 4.8. Query to list all captains who piloted ships built by general ship builders.

4.7.1 ON YOUR OWN EXERCISES

Write queries for on your own exercises 3.1 to 3.4 of Chapter 1.

```
1 •  select shipment.shipment_id
2    from shipment inner join ship on shipment.ship_no = ship.ship_no
3    inner join manufacturer on ship.manufacturer_id = manufacturer.manufacturer_id
4    where  manufacturer.name = 'General Ship Builders';
5
```

shipment_id
10-0004
11-0001

Figure 4.9. Query to list all shipments carried by ships built by general ship builders.

4.8   SHORE TO SHORE SHIPPING MAP

Please use the map in Figure 4.10 for your queries. Extra copies of the map can be downloaded from the book's website.

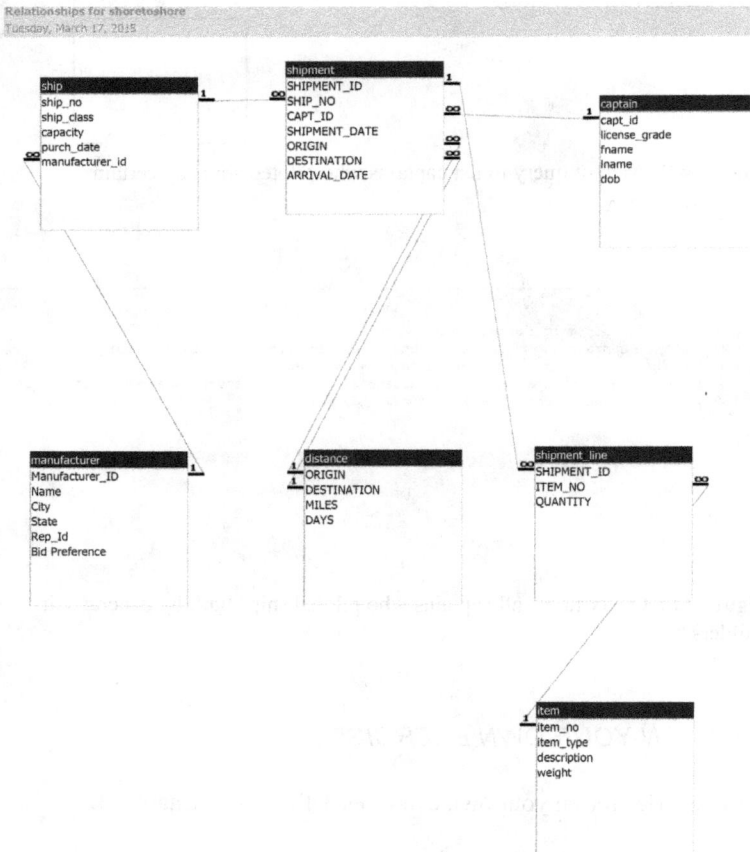

Figure 4.10. Map of entire case study for creating queries.

4.9 SUMMARY

In this chapter we looked at how to get data from more than one table using basic join operations. In the next chapter we will look at some more advanced join commands. In Chapter 6 we will look at using sub-queries, which is another way to extract data from multiple tables.

CHAPTER 5

ADVANCED JOIN OPERATIONS

5.1   INTRODUCTION

In Chapter 4, we looked at joining tables together in order to get the information that you need for a query. We discussed the inner join and also talked about the approach of using a map of the tables in order to find the path through the tables in order to obtain a query result. In this chapter we will look at some more advanced methods, namely self-joins and outer joins.

5.2   OBJECTIVES

- Review basic join operations
- Discuss self joins
- Introduce outer joins

5.3   REVIEW OF JOIN OPERATIONS

As you recall, there are many cases where we need to gather information from more than one table. A very basic join involves two tables that are joined by a common field. This common field is generally the primary key of one of the tables. As we add more tables to the select expression that executes the join, we find that there are generally n-1 join expressions in the where clause, where n is the number of tables. Let's look at another example.

Example 1: List all shipments that had John Smith as the captain.
It is clear that we have to join both the shipment table and the captain table, since only the capt_id is in the shipment table and we only have

```
1 •   select shipment.shipment_id
2     from shipment inner join captain
3     on shipment.capt_id = captain.capt_id
4     where captain.lname = 'Smith' and captain.fname ='John'
```

Result Grid | Filter Rows: | Export: | Wrap Cell Content:

shipment_id
▸ 10-0004
11-0004

Figure 5.1. Query to list all shipments with John Smith as captain.

```
1 •   select shipment.shipment_id
2     from shipment inner join ship on shipment.ship_no = ship.ship_no
3     inner join manufacturer on ship.manufacturer_id =
4     manufacturer.manufacturer_id
5     where manufacturer.name = 'General Ship Builders'
6
```

Result Grid | Filter Rows: | Export: | Wrap Cell Content:

shipment_id
▸ 10-0004
11-0001

Figure 5.2. Query to list all shipments carried by a ship built by general ship builders.

the captain's last name and first name as part of our where condition. The query for this is shown in Figure 5.1.

Let's look at another example where we will join three tables.

Example 2: List all shipments carried by a ship built by General Ship Builders

For this query, we must join the manufacturers table to the ship table and the ship table to the shipment table. The query is shown in Figure 5.2.

5.4   SELF JOINS

There are often cases where we want to compare information in the same table. There are two approaches to this: using a sub-query (which we will look at in detail in the next chapter) or a self join. Let's take a look at an example.

5.4.1   EXAMPLE 1

Find all captains who are older than Otheno Vollage.

One approach is to use a sub query:

select captain.lname,captain.fname
from captain
where dob > (select dob from captain where lname = 'Vollage' and
fname = 'Otheno');

We have not looked at sub-queries yet so I'll take a moment to explain.
More details on sub-queries can be found in Chapter 6.

A sub-query essentially runs first and the results are then used in
the outer query. In the previous example, the query in parenthesis (select
dob from captain where lname = 'Vollage' and fname = 'Otheno') will
return Otheno Vollage's date of birth. Anyone whose dob is after his will
be selected. So, the result from the sub-query is used to find records that
match the condition. We will see more of this in Chapter 6.

Another approach is to open the table up twice and give each instance
an alias as shown in Figure 5.3 below.

Both queries would return the same result set. The second query
would be more efficient since the sub query does not have to be run for
every row.

5.4.2 EXAMPLE 2

Find all shipments that had the same origin as either shipment 09-0001 or
09-0002.

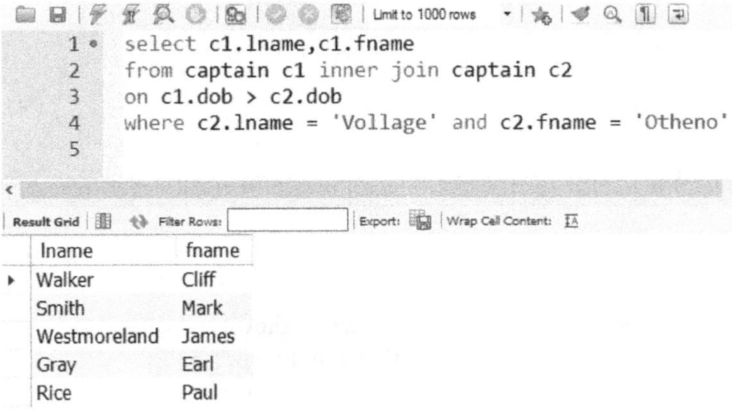

Figure 5.3. Sample self-join query to find all captains older than Otheno
vollage.

```
1 •  select shipment_id
2    from shipment
3    where origin in (select origin from shipment where shipment_id in ('09-0001','09-0002'))
4    and shipment_id not in ('09-0001','09-0002');
5
6
```

shipment_id
▸ 09-0005
11-0001
10-0001
10-0003
10-0004
11-0003
11-0005
10-0002
11-0004

Figure 5.4. Query to find all shipments that had same origin as shipment 09-0001 or shipment 09-0002 using a sub-query.

```
1 •  select s1.shipment_id
2    from shipment s1 inner join shipment s2
3    on s1.origin = s2.origin
4    where s2.shipment_id in ('09-0001','09-0002')
5    and s2.shipment_id <> s1.shipment_id;
6
```

shipment_id
▸ 10-0002
11-0004
09-0005
11-0001
10-0001
10-0003
10-0004
11-0003
11-0005

Figure 5.5. Query to find all shipments that had same origin as shipment 09-0001 or shipment 09-0002 using a self-join.

Again, here we could use a sub-query as shown in Figure 5.4.

Or, we could use a self join as shown in Figure 5.5.

A couple of things to note here. Notice that in both examples, we are not joining on a primary key. Also, notice that the join operator is not necessarily always an equals. In the second example, we need some means to eliminate duplicates.

5.4.3 ON YOUR OWN EXERCISES

5.1. List item numbers and descriptions for all items that are of the same type as beans.

5.2. Find all shipments where the origin is the same as any shipments where John Smith was the captain.

5.5 OUTER JOINS

The join operations that we have looked at so far are called inner joins. Let's look at an example.

Notice that only the ship numbers of ships that carried shipments are shown. However, suppose that we wanted to display all ships, regardless of whether or not they ever were used for a shipment. In addition, for those that were used for a shipment, we want to list the shipment_id of that shipment. This can be accomplished with an outer join. There are three types of outer joins: left outer joins, right outer joins and full outer joins. One thing to keep in mind is that there are a couple of different standards for writing these. In this text, I will present the SQL-99 Ansi standard. Let's look at some examples.

5.5.1 LEFT OUTER JOIN

In our example in Figure 5.6, there may be some cases where we want to list ships that have not been used for a shipment. This is called a left outer join, since we are retaining all of the rows from the left table, regardless of whether or not they have a corresponding row in the right table. Figure 5.7 shows this query.

Note in the figure that the bottom line (ship 35) has a null for a shipment id.

5.5.2 RIGHT OUTER JOIN

Now, there might also be cases where we want to display all rows in the right table regardless of whether or not there is a corresponding row in the left table. This is called a right outer join. Let's look at an example, Figure 5.8.

Notice that the very last captain in the list, Phillip Levenchuck, has no shipments.

The choice of when to use a left outer join versus a right outer join mostly depends upon how you wish to order the join operation. When you

```
1 •  select ship.ship_no, shipment.shipment_id
2    from ship inner join shipment
3    on ship.ship_no = shipment.ship_no
```

ship_no	shipment_id
▶ 25	09-0001
1	09-0002
11	09-0003
5	09-0004
1	09-0005
1	10-0001
5	10-0002
11	10-0003
39	10-0004
39	11-0001
37	11-0002
10	11-0003
16	11-0004
5	11-0005
6	11-0006

Figure 5.6. Query to list shipment_ID and ship_no using an inner join.

```
1 •  select ship.ship_no, shipment.shipment_id
2    from ship left outer join shipment
3    on ship.ship_no = shipment.ship_no
```

ship_no	shipment_id
▶ 25	09-0001
1	09-0002
11	09-0003
5	09-0004
1	09-0005
1	10-0001
5	10-0002
11	10-0003
39	10-0004
39	11-0001
37	11-0002
10	11-0003
16	11-0004
5	11-0005
6	11-0006
35	NULL

Figure 5.7. Query to list shipment_ID and ship_no using a left outer join.

```
1 •   select shipment_id,lname,fname
2     from shipment right outer join captain
3     on shipment.capt_id = captain.capt_id
```

Result Grid		Filter Rows:		Export:	Wrap Cell Content:

shipment_id	lname	fname
09-0001	Smith	Mark
09-0002	Rice	Paul
09-0003	Westmoreland	James
09-0004	Levine	Sal
09-0005	Moore	Henry
10-0001	Walker	Cliff
10-0002	Sourchie	Robert
10-0003	Levine	Sal
10-0004	Smith	John
11-0001	Moore	Henry
11-0002	Vollage	Otheno
11-0003	Westmoreland	James
11-0004	Smith	John
11-0005	Nesmith	Marcia
11-0006	Gray	Earl
NULL	Levinchuck	Phillip

Figure 5.8. Query to list captains for all shipments using right outer join.

```
select shipment.ship_no,shipment_line.shipment_id,item.item_no,item.description
from shipment_line right outer join item
on shipment_line.item_no = item.item_no
inner join shipment
  on shipment_line.shipment_id
= shipment.shipment_id
```

Figure 5.9. Query of all items regardless of whether they shipped or not using outer and inner joins.

begin to use an outer join in multiple table joins, things can get a bit tricky. Sometimes we mix outer joins with inner joins. The thing to keep in mind is that once you reach a part of a query where a null value is not carried forward then you lose the row. For example, suppose that you would like to list all items (regardless of whether or not they shipped) along with the ship_no and capacity of all ships that shipped any item that was shipped. For this query, we must add the shipment table, since ship_no is not in the shipment_line table. The query is shown in Figure 5.9 and the results in Figure 5.10.

ship_no	shipment_id	item_no	description
25	09-0001	3223	Concrete Forms
25	09-0001	3297	Steel Beam
25	09-0001	3299	Small Steel Plate
1	09-0002	3212	Cement
1	09-0002	3223	Concrete Forms
11	09-0003	2101	Beans
11	09-0003	2109	Corn Meal
11	09-0003	2123	Rice
11	09-0003	2125	Oats
5	09-0004	3212	Cement
5	09-0004	3223	Concrete Forms
1	09-0005	3297	Steel Beam
1	09-0005	7821	Toyota Camry
1	09-0005	7823	Mercury Sable
1	10-0001	7821	Toyota Camry
1	10-0001	7829	Mercedes
1	10-0001	7830	Honda Accord
5	10-0002	4521	5/8" Plywood - 200 sheets/pallet
5	10-0002	4532	Beam
5	10-0002	4533	2X4X8 Pine Boards
11	10-0003	4521	5/8" Plywood - 200 sheets/pallet
11	10-0003	4534	3/4" Plywood - 200 sheets/pallet
39	10-0004	2101	Beans
39	10-0004	2109	Corn Meal
39	10-0004	2125	Oats
39	11-0001	4521	5/8" Plywood - 200 sheets/pallet
39	11-0001	4532	Beam
37	11-0002	4533	2X4X8 Pine Boards
37	11-0002	4534	3/4" Plywood - 200 sheets/pallet
10	11-0003	7829	Mercedes
16	11-0004	3223	Concrete Forms
16	11-0004	3297	Steel Beam
5	11-0005	2101	Beans
5	11-0005	2109	Corn Meal
6	11-0006	2125	Oats
6	11-0006	7830	Honda Accord

Figure 5.10. Results of Figure 5.9 query.

Notice that items 2126, 4527, and 7831 do not appear in our list at all. These are all items that have never been shipped. Let's look a little bit further to dissect what happened and how to fix it. Let's split the statement into two separate ones. Let's first join shipment_line to item:

select shipment_id,item.item_no

from shipment_line right outer join item
on shipment_line.item_no = item.item_no

The results are shown in Table 5.1.

Notice that the shipment_id for the last three lines is null. For the purpose of the next statement, let's assume that the data in Table 5.1 is named sl_item. We would write:

Table 5.1. Results of query to join shipment_line to item

Shipment_ID	Item_No
09-0001	3223
09-0001	3297
09-0001	3299
09-0002	3212
09-0002	3223
09-0003	2101
09-0003	2109
09-0003	2123
09-0003	2125
09-0004	3212
09-0004	3223
09-0005	3297
09-0005	7821
09-0005	7823
10-0001	7821
10-0001	7829
10-0001	7830
10-0002	4521
10-0002	4532
10-0002	4533
10-0003	4521
10-0003	4534
10-0004	2101
10-0004	2109
10-0004	2125

(Continued)

Table 5.1. (Continued)

11-0001	4521
11-0001	4532
11-0002	4533
11-0002	4534
11-0003	7829
11-0004	3223
11-0004	3297
11-0005	2101
11-0005	2109
11-0006	2125
11-0006	7830
Null	2126
Null	4527
Null	7831

Select shipment.ship_no, sl.shipment_id.sl.item_no
from shipment inner join sl on shipment.shipment_id = sl.shipment_id

Since an inner join only matches rows that match the join condition there is no null shipment_id in shipment, so the last three rows are discarded. To fix this we need to be consistent with the joins. If we rewrite the preceding query as:

select shipment.ship_no, sl.shipment_id.sl.item_no
from shipment right outer join sl on shipment.shipment_id =
sl.shipment_id

We will then end up with the last three items appearing in our result set. Let's rewrite the original query:

select shipment.ship_no,shipment_line.shipment_id,item.item_no
from shipment_line right outer join item
on shipment_line.item_no = item.item_no
left outer join shipment
on shipment_line.shipment_id
= shipment.shipment_id;

One thing to note here is that I did switch to a left outer join for the second join. This is because everything to the *left* of shipment could

Table 5.2. Results from rewritten query with consistent outer join

Ship_No	Shipment_ID	Item_No
25	09-0001	3223
25	09-0001	3297
25	09-0001	3299
1	09-0002	3212
1	09-0002	3223
11	09-0003	2101
11	09-0003	2109
11	09-0003	2123
11	09-0003	2125
5	09-0004	3212
5	09-0004	3223
1	09-0005	3297
1	09-0005	7821
1	09-0005	7823
1	10-0001	7821
1	10-0001	7829
1	10-0001	7830
5	10-0002	4521
5	10-0002	4532
5	10-0002	4533
11	10-0003	4521
11	10-0003	4534
39	10-0004	2101
39	10-0004	2109
39	10-0004	2125
39	11-0001	4521
39	11-0001	4532
37	11-0002	4533
37	11-0002	4534
10	11-0003	7829
16	11-0004	3223
16	11-0004	3297

(Continued)

Table 5.2. (Continued)

5	11-0005	2101
5	11-0005	2109
6	11-0006	2125
6	11-0006	7830
		2126
		4527
		7831

include a nonmatching value. The best way to make sure that you are writing these queries correctly is to test them and validate the results.

The results of this query are shown in Table 5.2.

5.5.3 ON YOUR OWN EXERCISES

2.1. List all captains (lname and fname) and the shipment_id for each shipment that the captain piloted. Also, list all captains who have had no shipments.

2.2. List all shipment ids for each origin/destination pair in the distance table. Include origin/destination pairs that have had no shipments.

2.3. Find all shipments that do not have a shipment line.

5.6 SUMMARY

In this chapter we explored join operations in further depth, particularly self joins and outer joins. In Chapter 6, we will look at one other method for gathering data from multiple tables.

CHAPTER 6

Sᴜʙ-ǫᴜᴇʀɪᴇꜱ

6.1   INTRODUCTION

We have looked at how to join tables using various join operations. While in most cases these will work just fine to get the desired result, there are cases where we have to use a sub-query. In this chapter we will look at a way to query multiple tables using a sub-query.

6.2   OBJECTIVES

- Discuss relational operators
- Show the use of IN and Not IN operators
- Discuss when to use the Exists and Not Exists operators
- Examine correlated Sub-queries

6.3   SUB-QUERIES

SQL syntax allows for the use of sub-queries as part of the where clause as well as a means to specify a virtual table. We will not discuss using sub-queries for virtual tables in this chapter. Sub-queries can be used in the where clause to gather a group of records that might meet a certain condition. We can use any of the relational operators ($<$, $<=$, $=$, $>$, $>=$, $<>$) as well as in. Let's look at an example: find all ships where the capacity is equal to the capacity of ship 39. Here we could use the $=$ operator with a subquery. The query would be written as shown in Figure 6.1.

Now that you know a bit about join operations, you may have recognized that this query could have been written using a self-join. Many sub-queries could be written using joins, except in a few cases. All queries in relational database management systems are run through a query

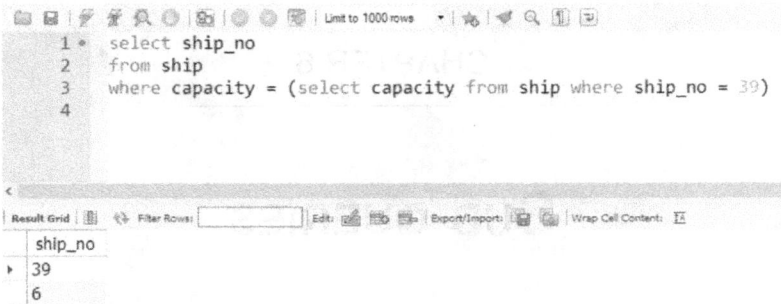

Figure 6.1. Query to find all ships with capacity equal to capacity of ship 39.

processor, so in many cases a sub-query will execute the same as a join. One rule of thumb that I have with sub-queries: nesting a lot of subqueries together is harder to debug and understand. In this case, I would recommend using joins.

Of course we might want to eliminate ship number 39 from the result set, so we could rewrite this as follows:

```
select ship_no
from ship
where capacity = (select capacity from ship where ship_no = 39)
and ship_no != 39
```

We could also find all ships that have a capacity not equal to the capacity of ship number 39:

```
select ship_no
from ship
where capacity != (select capacity from ship where ship_no= 39)
```

We could also use any of the other operators such as less than, greater than, and so on. Let's take a look at one more example: find all ships that have a capacity greater than or equal to the average capacity of all ships. Here we can use the average operator to find the average capacity. If we write the subquery first, it will look like the following:

```
select avg(capacity) from ship
and return 168500.
```

We can now write the main query for this, as shown in Figure 6.2.

```
1   select ship_no
2   from ship
3   where capacity >= (select avg(capacity) from ship)
```

Result Grid | Filter Rows: | Edit: | Export/Import: | Wrap Cell Cont

ship_no
▸ 37
39
6

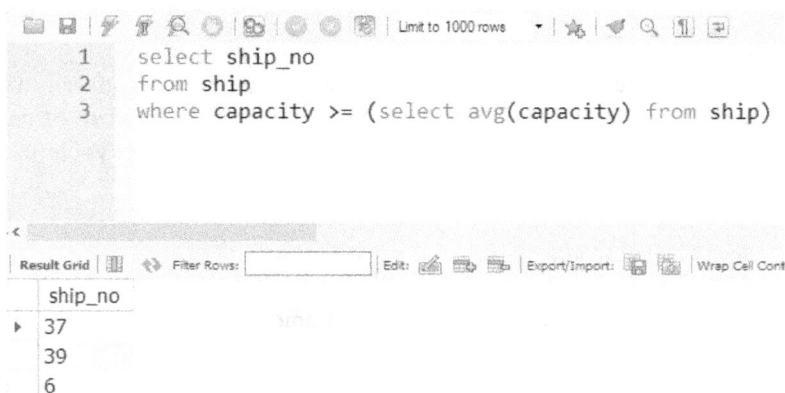

Figure 6.2. Query to find all ships with capacity greater than or equal to average capacity of all ships.

This particular query has to be done using a sub-query.

One use of sub-queries is to perform a join through the use of the in operator. The in operator simply specifies that the query should return only records that are *in* the sub-query. Let's rewrite a join query (find the name of the manufacturer of ship 37) with a sub-query rather than using a join condition:

Original query:
select manufacturer.name
from manufacturer,ship
where manufacturer.manufacturer_id = ship.manufacturer_id
and ship.ship_no = 37;

Query using sub-query:
select name
from manufacturer
where manufacturer_id = (select manufacturer_id
from ship where ship_no = 37);

As you can see, this is slightly different from the first query using the join. Instead of joining the two tables, we find the manufacturer_id first and then find the manufacturer with that manufacturer_id. We could have also used the in operator here. However, since the sub-query only returned one value, we could also use the = operator. While this method works fine for two tables, it can quickly get messy with more than two tables. Also, it is less efficient since the RDBMS needs to execute the sub-query for every row of the manufacturer table until a match is found. In this case, it is trivial since the tables are small.

The in operator is useful for cases where there are multiple rows returned from a sub-query. For example, if we wanted to find all of the captains who piloted shipments that originated in Boston, we could use the in operator as follows:

> select lname,fname
> from captain
> where capt_id in (select capt_id from shipment where origin
>   = 'BOSTON');

Again, this query could have also been written through the use of a join. However, there is a case where we could not use a join. Suppose that we would like to find all captains who have *never* been the captain of a shipment that originated in Boston. The natural tendency is to write this query as follows:

> select captain.lname, captain.fname
> from captain, shipment
> where captain.capt_id !=shipment.capt_id
> and origin = 'BOSTON';

However, when we run this we get a result set of 88 rows. We cannot use the != operator here. The RDBMS is going to then match every row of captain that does not match the capt_id of each row of shipment. In this case, we *must* use a sub-query. We can add a *not* to the *in* operator and rewrite the query as shown in Figure 6.3.

When we run this, we get back a result set of five records.

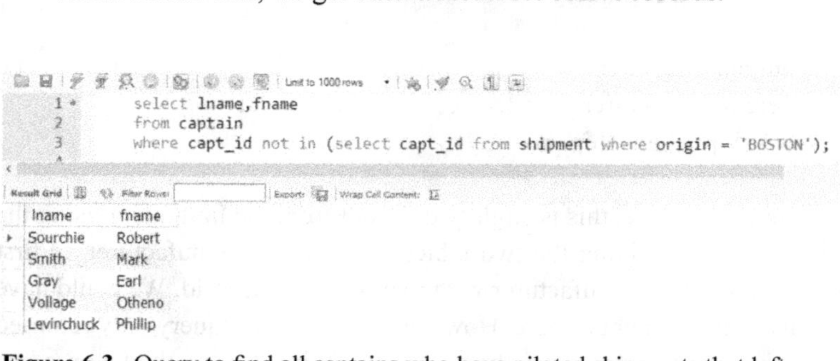

Figure 6.3. Query to find all captains who have piloted shipments that left Boston.

6.3.1 ON YOUR OWN EXERCISES

1.1 List any manufacturers who did not sell a ship to Shore to Shore. (Hint: make a list of all manufacturer IDS in the ship table and then list all manufacturers who are not in that list.)

6.3.2 CORRELATED SUBQUERIES USING EXISTS

Sometimes, it may be necessary to write a subquery that uses data from the outer query as a condition of the subquery. One way to do this is with the exists predicate. The exists predicate (which can also be combined with not) returns a boolean result: either the subquery produced results or it did not. Let's look at an example.

6.3.3 EXAMPLE

List all items that have shipped. The query is shown in Figure 6.4.

As you can see, this is not very different from the in operator. The major difference here is that we are using the outer query in the inner subquery. Also, note that the table for the outer query is not referenced at

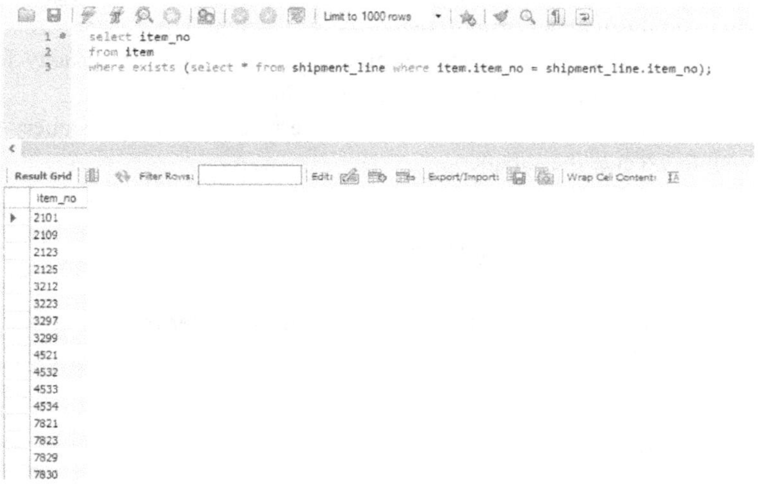

Figure 6.4. Query to list all items that have shipped using correlated sub-query.

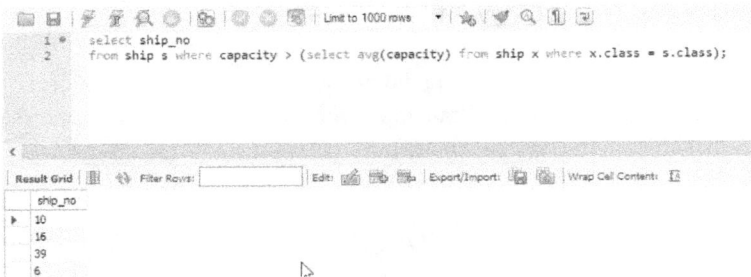

Figure 6.5. Query to list ships with a capacity greater than the average capacity for their class using a correlated sub-query.

all in the subquery. One other thing to note about correlated subqueries is that they are resource intensive because each row of the outer table has to run the sub-query. This is much different from using a relational operator or the in operator. In these cases, the sub-query (called the inner query) is run once and then the outer query runs. Keep this in mind when designing queries.

6.3.4 OTHER CORRELATED SUBQUERIES

Another case where you might want to use a correlated subquery is to compare a table to itself using some aggregation, such as average. You cannot do this with a self-join. Let's look at an example.

List all ships with a capacity greater than the average capacity for their class. The query and results are shown in Figure 6.5.

As you can see from this example, every row of the outer query is going to execute the subquery.

6.3.5 ON YOUR OWN EXERCISES

2.1 Use a correlated sub-query to find all ships greater than the average weight for their class.

6.4 SUMMARY

In this chapter, we looked at the use of sub-queries using relational operators, the in/not in operators and correlated sub-queries.

CHAPTER 7

GROUPING DATA

7.1 INTRODUCTION

We have spent the last several chapters looking at how to retrieve data from multiple tables. There may also be times when we want to group data together. For example, perhaps for each captain we would like to know how many shipments he or she was the captain of. In this chapter, we will look at grouping data. We will also take a look at inline views, one way to use the grouped data in another query.

7.2 OBJECTIVES

- Introduce the group by clause
- Discuss group by with the having clause
- Explain the use of count distinct
- Discuss inline views and how they can be used for adding aggregate grouped data to a query

7.3 THE GROUP BY CLAUSE

So far, we have looked at aggregation and counts for the entire table. However, there often is a need to combine several rows that have a common value for a field. In order to do this, we can use the group by clause. Let's look at an example.

7.3.1 EXAMPLE 7.1

Management would like a report of the number of shipments for each captain. The report should list the captain's name and the number of

```
1 •      select count(shipment_id)
2        from captain inner join shipment
3        on captain.capt_id = shipment.capt_id
```

Result Grid | Filter Rows: | Export: | Wrap Cell Content: IA

count(shipment_id)
15

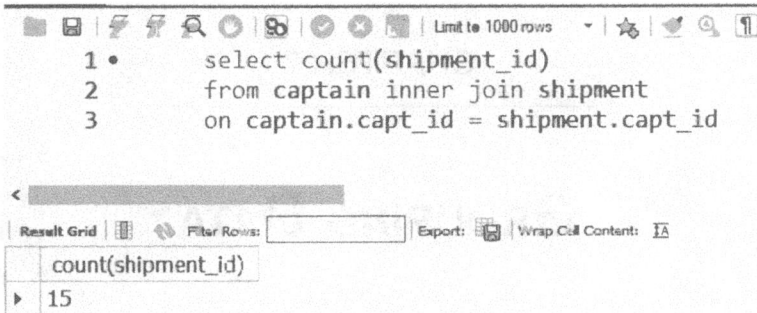

Figure 7.1. Query to list number of shipments for all captains.

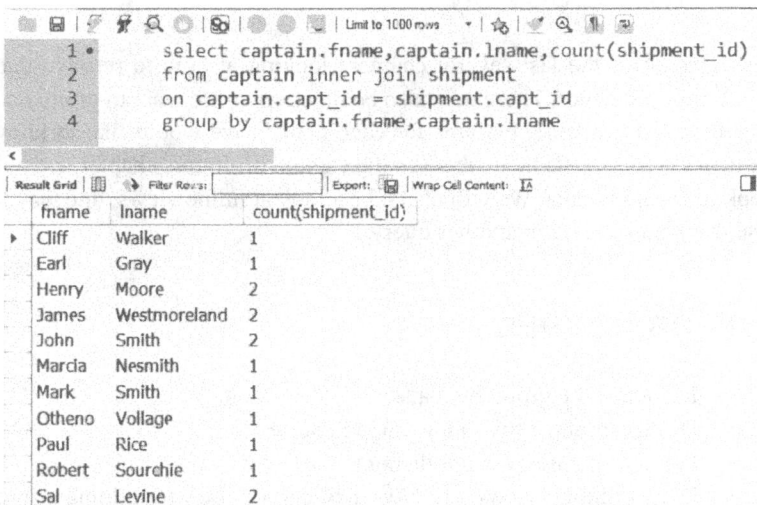

```
1 •      select captain.fname,captain.lname,count(shipment_id)
2        from captain inner join shipment
3        on captain.capt_id = shipment.capt_id
4        group by captain.fname,captain.lname
```

Result Grid | Filter Rows: | Export: | Wrap Cell Content: IA

fname	lname	count(shipment_id)
Cliff	Walker	1
Earl	Gray	1
Henry	Moore	2
James	Westmoreland	2
John	Smith	2
Marcia	Nesmith	1
Mark	Smith	1
Otheno	Vollage	1
Paul	Rice	1
Robert	Sourchie	1
Sal	Levine	2

Figure 7.2. Query to list number of shipments for each captain using group by clause.

shipments. Our first thought might be to use just the count(*) or count(shipment_id) as shown in the query in Figure 7.1.

However, notice that this only produces the total number of shipments that had captains. Let's use the group by clause to produce the desired results, as shown in Figure 7.2.

7.3.2 GROUP BY SYNTAX

The group by clause is simply added to the end of your select statement. The select statement syntax now can be expressed as follows:

```
select{exp1,exp2,...,expn}
from {table1,table2,...tablen}
[where {condition}]
[group by {exp1, exp2, ...expn}]
[order by {exp1,exp2,...,expn}];
```

The group by clause can include more than one expression that can define the groups. The expressions are usually a column returned in the result set of the query, although they do not have to even be specified in the first line of the select statement. We can think of the group by clause as acting similar to a break statement in a report. Essentially, the initial query is executed and the result set is sorted on the group by expression. If we are simply counting rows, then the RDBMS keeps track of the rows until the expression changes. At this point, the expression and the count are returned and the next group is processed. The same process occurs with the sum aggregate function, except a numeric value is added to a summation variable until the group changes. The max, min, and average operate in a similar fashion.

7.3.3   EXAMPLE 7.2

The group by expression can perform other aggregate functions. For example, let's say that we want to compute the total distance that each ship has traveled, as shown in Figure 7.3.

```
1 •  select shipment.ship_no,sum(distance.miles)
2    from shipment inner join distance
3    on shipment.origin = distance.origin
4    and shipment.destination = distance.destination
5    group by shipment.ship_no
```

Result Grid | Filter Rows: | Export: | Wrap Cell Content:

ship_no	sum(distance.miles)
1	10500.00
10	6000.00
11	5600.00
16	9000.00
25	6000.00
37	2600.00
39	5500.00
5	24000.00
6	9000.00

Figure 7.3. Query to find total distance traveled for each ship.

```
1 •  select shipment.ship_no,sum(distance.miles) as totdist,
2         avg(distance.miles) as avgdist,
3         max(distance.miles) as maxdist,
4         min(distance.miles) as mindist
5
6    from shipment inner join distance
7    on shipment.origin = distance.origin
8    and shipment.destination = distance.destination
9    group by shipment.ship_no
```

ship_no	totdist	avgdist	maxdist	mindist
1	10500.00	3500.000000	5000.00	2500.00
10	6000.00	6000.000000	6000.00	6000.00
11	5600.00	2800.000000	3000.00	2600.00
16	9000.00	9000.000000	9000.00	9000.00
25	6000.00	6000.000000	6000.00	6000.00
37	2600.00	2600.000000	2600.00	2600.00
39	5500.00	2750.000000	3000.00	2500.00
5	24000.00	8000.000000	9000.00	6000.00
6	9000.00	9000.000000	9000.00	9000.00

Figure 7.4. Query to find total, average, maximum and minimum distance traveled for each ship.

We could also expand this example to include the total distance, average distance, maximum distance of any one shipment and minimum distance of any one ship as shown in Figure 7.4.

Notice that we have renamed the fields in order to conserve space.

7.4   CALCULATED FIELDS

It may be necessary to perform a calculation as part of a group by. One example would be to calculate the total price of an item. Let's look at an example.

7.4.1   EXAMPLE 7.3

We looked at an example in a prior chapter to list the total weight for shipment number 09-0001 As you recall, the shipment_line table contains multiple lines with the same shipment_id, one for each item. Clearly, this query must be done with a group by in order to calculate the total weight of the shipment. Each shipment_line has a quantity which must be multiplied by the item weight. In this case, we also will use the where clause in order to specify that we only want to look at the results for shipment 09-0001. Figure 7.5 shows the query as well as the results.

Notice that we did not include the shipment_id in the first line of the select. This is because we do not need to display the shipment_id. We can modify this query to show the total weight of each shipment by removing the where clause and adding shipment_id to the select expression. The query and results are shown in Figure 7.6.

```
select sum(shipment_line.quantity * item.weight)
from shipment_line inner join item
on shipment_line.item_no = item.item_no
where shipment_id = '09-0001'
group by shipment_id
```

sum(shipment_line.quantity * item.weight)
249500.00

Figure 7.5. Query to calculate total weight of shipment 09-0001.

```
select shipment_id,sum(shipment_line.quantity * item.weight)
from shipment_line inner join item
on shipment_line.item_no = item.item_no
group by shipment_id
```

shipment_id	sum(shipment_line.quantity * item.weight)
09-0001	249500.00
09-0002	225000.00
09-0003	493200.00
09-0004	22500.00
09-0005	206500.00
10-0001	223650.00
10-0002	340000.00
10-0003	440000.00
10-0004	678760.00
11-0001	18000.00
11-0002	43000.00
11-0003	2550000.00
11-0004	95000.00
11-0005	250000.00
11-0006	174375.00

Figure 7.6. Query to calculate total weight of each shipment using group by clause.

7.4.2   ON YOUR OWN EXERCISES

1.1 For each item, list the total quantity shipped to date.
1.2 For each item, list the total quantity shipped to date on class 1 ships.
1.3 For each ship, list the average distance traveled for all shipments of building materials shipped on the ship.

7.5   GROUP BY WITH THE HAVING CLAUSE

There is an additional clause that can be added to the group by clause, called having. Having is like the where clause, except that it acts on the grouped result set returned. Let's look at an example.

7.5.1   EXAMPLE 7.3

Let's rework example 7.1 to include only captains who had more than 1 shipment. The query is shown in Figure 7.7.

As you can see, the having clause is working only on the result set after the group by has been performed. Many people get confused between the having and the where clause. The where clause *only operates on a single row at a time* whereas the having clause operates on the grouped result set. The having can be used for any operation (count, sum, average, min, max, and so on). Let's take a look at an example:

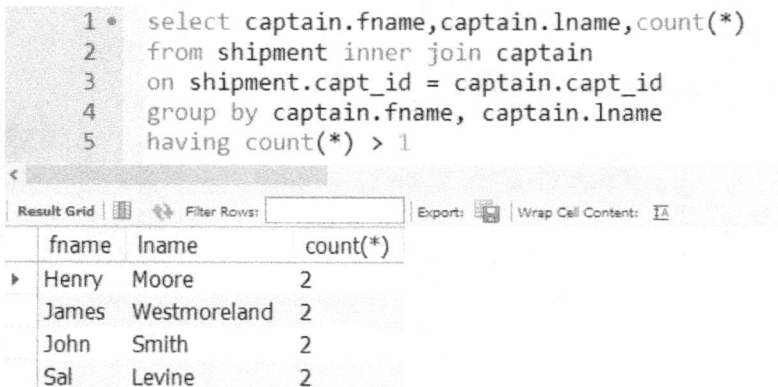

```
1 • select captain.fname,captain.lname,count(*)
2   from shipment inner join captain
3   on shipment.capt_id = captain.capt_id
4   group by captain.fname, captain.lname
5   having count(*) > 1
```

fname	lname	count(*)
Henry	Moore	2
James	Westmoreland	2
John	Smith	2
Sal	Levine	2

Figure 7.7. Query to show count of shipments by captain for captains with more than one shipment.

```
1    select ship_no,sum(distance.miles)
2    from shipment inner join distance
3    on shipment.origin = distance.origin
4    and shipment.destination = distance.destination
5    group by shipment.ship_no
6    having sum(miles) > 6000
```

Result Grid		Filter Rows:	Export:	Wrap Cell Content:
ship_no	sum(distance.miles)
1	10500.00
10	6000.00
11	5600.00
16	9000.00
25	6000.00
37	2600.00
39	5500.00
5	24000.00
6	9000.00

Figure 7.8. Query to calculate distance for each shipment with a distance of more than 6000 miles.

7.5.2 EXAMPLE 7.4

Let's rework example 7.2 to find only ships that have traveled more than 6,000 miles. The query and results are shown in Figure 7.8.

7.5.3 ON YOUR OWN EXERCISES

2.1 Find the weight of all shipments that are more than 10,000 pounds
2.2 Find all origin-destination pairs that had more than two shipments

7.6 USING COUNT DISTINCT

For most group by queries where you want to produce a count, using count(*) works just fine. We have seen several queries in this chapter that use count(*). However, there are cases where multiple values are returned in the result set for one field. This is not necessarily wrong, but this will cause your count to be off. Let's look at an example.

7.6.1 EXAMPLE 7.5

We need to list out each captain and also the number of shipments that he or she was captain of that carried building materials (item_type = 'BL'). Let's first write this using count(*) and grouping on fname and lname. The query and results are shown in Figure 7.9.

Let's dig a little deeper into the data. Figure 7.10 shows a query with the data before the group by.

One thing that you will notice is that there are multiple lines for each captain for the same shipment. This is because there can be more than one item of type "BL" in a shipment. Since we need to join through shipment_ line, the results are being counted. Each *row* of the result set goes into the count. We can work around this by using count distinct with the specific field that we wish to count (in this case shipment_line.shipment_id). This will eliminate duplicate rows with the same shipment_id and different items. Figure 7.11 shows the query as well as the results.

7.7   COUNT DISTINCT AND OUTER JOINS

There is also one special case where you need to use count distinct with outer joins. Let's rework example 7.5 to take into account any captains who never had shipments. The results should show the count as zero.

```
1 •  select fname,lname,count(*)
2    from captain inner join shipment
3    on captain.capt_id = shipment.capt_id
4    inner join shipment_line
5    on shipment.shipment_id = shipment_line.shipment_id
6    inner join item
7    on shipment_line.item_no = item.item_no
8    where item_type = 'BL'
9    group by fname,lname
```

Result Grid   Filter Rows: Export: Wrap Cell Contents

fname	lname	count(*)
Henry	Moore	1
John	Smith	2
Mark	Smith	3
Paul	Rice	2
Sal	Levine	2

Figure 7.9. Count distinct example—count of shipments that carried building materials by each captain.

```
1 • select fname,lname,shipment.shipment_id,item.item_no
2   from captain inner join shipment
3   on captain.capt_id = shipment.capt_id
4   inner join shipment_line
5   on shipment.shipment_id = shipment_line.shipment_id
6   inner join item
7   on shipment_line.item_no = item.item_no
8   where item_type = 'BL';
```

fname	lname	shipment_id	item_no
Mark	Smith	09-0001	3223
Mark	Smith	09-0001	3297
Mark	Smith	09-0001	3299
Paul	Rice	09-0002	3212
Paul	Rice	09-0002	3223
Sal	Levine	09-0004	3212
Sal	Levine	09-0004	3223
Henry	Moore	09-0005	3297
John	Smith	11-0004	3223
John	Smith	11-0004	3297

Figure 7.10. Query of individual shipments by captain.

```
1 • select fname,lname,count(distinct shipment_line.shipment_id)
2   from captain inner join shipment
3   on captain.capt_id = shipment.capt_id
4   inner join shipment_line
5   on shipment.shipment_id = shipment_line.shipment_id
6   inner join item
7   on shipment_line.item_no = item.item_no
8   where item_type = 'BL'
9   group by fname,lname
```

fname	lname	count(distinct shipment_line.shipment_id)
Henry	Moore	1
John	Smith	1
Mark	Smith	1
Paul	Rice	1
Sal	Levine	1

Figure 7.11. Count distinct query plus results.

We know from examining the tables and our work with the case study that there is one captain, Phillip Levinchuck, who has never had a shipment. Let's rework the last set of queries to use an outer join. We will count all

Figure 7.12. Query example: Count with outer join.

shipments for captains without worrying about item_type. The query and results are shown in Figure 7.12.

When you look at Phillip Levinchuck's record in the result set, you will see a count of 1. This is not correct because the query is only counting rows returned even if the row had a null value. In order to fix this we need to use a count distinct. Figure 7.13 shows the query along with the results.

7.8 INLINE VIEWS

Some of the result sets that are created by using the group by clause are useful as part of other larger queries. However, due to the nature of the group by clause, you cannot try to join multiple tables and only group by some of the results. A good example of this is calculating the weight of each shipment. We can do this with the query shown in Figure 7.14. This might be useful later on as part of a larger query or to compare the results.

```
1 •  select fname,lname,count(distinct shipment_id)
2    from captain left outer join shipment
3    on captain.capt_id = shipment.capt_id
4    group by fname,lname
```

Result Grid | Filter Rows: | Export: | Wrap Cell Content: |

fname	lname	count(distinct shipment_id)
▶ Cliff	Walker	1
Earl	Gray	1
Henry	Moore	2
James	Westmoreland	2
John	Smith	2
Marcia	Nesmith	1
Mark	Smith	1
Otheno	Vollage	1
Paul	Rice	1
Phillip	Levinchuck	0
Robert	Sourchie	1
Sal	Levine	2

Figure 7.13. Count distinct with outer join example.

```
select ┌shipment_id,sum(quantity*weight)
from shipment_line inner join item
on shipment_line.item_no = item.item_no
group by shipment_id;
```

Query Result ×

SQL | All Rows Fetched: 15 in 0.01 seconds

	SHIPMENT_ID	SUM(QUANTITY*WEIGHT)
1	10-0002	340000
2	11-0003	2550000
3	10-0004	678760
4	09-0002	225000
5	10-0001	223650
6	09-0003	493200
7	09-0001	249500
8	11-0005	250000
9	09-0005	206500
10	11-0006	174375
11	09-0004	22500
12	11-0004	95000
13	10-0003	440000
14	11-0001	18000
15	11-0002	43000

Figure 7.14. Query to calculate the weight of each shipment with results.

```
 1 •  select shipment.shipment_id, captain.lname,captain.fname,origin,destination,
 2          shipment.shipment_date,sm_weight.totweight
 3    from shipment inner join captain
 4      on shipment.capt_id = captain.capt_id
 5    ⊟inner join (select shipment_id, sum(quantity*weight) as totweight
 6      from shipment_line inner join item
 7      on shipment_line.item_no = item.item_no
 8     ⌐group by shipment_id) sm_weight
 9      on shipment.shipment_id = sm_weight.shipment_id
```

shipment_id	lname	fname	origin	destination	shipment_date	totweight
09-0001	Smith	Mark	SEATTLE	BOSTON	2016-03-12	249500.00
09-0002	Rice	Paul	BOSTON	SINGAPORE	2016-04-15	225000.00
09-0003	Westmoreland	James	BRAZIL	BOSTON	2016-06-01	493200.00
09-0004	Levine	Sal	LONDON	SEATTLE	2016-07-10	22500.00
09-0005	Moore	Henry	BOSTON	BRAZIL	2016-09-19	206500.00
10-0001	Walker	Cliff	BOSTON	LONDON	2017-01-15	223650.00
10-0002	Sourchie	Robert	SEATTLE	LONDON	2017-01-15	340000.00
10-0003	Levine	Sal	BOSTON	LONDON	2017-01-18	440000.00
10-0004	Smith	John	BOSTON	LONDON	2017-03-13	678760.00
11-0001	Moore	Henry	BOSTON	BRAZIL	2018-06-10	18000.00
11-0002	Vollage	Otheno	BRAZIL	BOSTON	2018-07-15	43000.00
11-0003	Westmoreland	James	BOSTON	SEATTLE	2018-08-20	2550000.00
11-0004	Smith	John	SEATTLE	LONDON	2018-09-01	95000.00
11-0005	Nesmith	Marcia	BOSTON	SEATTLE	2018-09-15	250000.00
11-0006	Gray	Earl	LONDON	SEATTLE	2018-09-17	174375.00

Figure 7.15. Query to calculate the weight of each shipment using Inline view.

We could save this as a view, which is a virtual table updated dynamically as the underlying data changes. Another option is to create an inline view. In SQL, one can create a table from a select statement. Let's show the captain's name, the origin and destination, shipment date as well as the total weight of the shipment for all shipments. The query with the results is shown in Figure 7.15.

A couple of things to take note of here:

1. We had to give the inline view an alias in order to reference it in the select expression
2. We had to name the sum(weight*quantity) in order to be able to create the inline view

Unlike a stored view, the inline view is only available during the query. It is deleted right after the query finishes executing.

7.8.1   ON YOUR OWN EXERCISES

3.1 Write a query to show for each shipment the total weight of the shipment, the shipment_id, the ship number and the capacity of the ship.

7.9 SUMMARY

In this chapter we looked at the group by clause, which is a very power-ful tool to use in order to generate aggregate data. We also examined the having clause, which is like a where clause but applied to the entire group in a group by clause. We also looked at inline views and how these can be used to incorporate the results of group by queries in larger queries.

About the Author

John Russo is Associate Professor of Computer Science at Landmark College in Putney Vermont. He has been teaching for over 20 years in computer science programs at several colleges and engineering institutions. He also works as a computer scientist on large scale database management systems used in epidemiological research. Prior to his career in academia, he worked in a variety of roles in industry for 15 years.

INDEX

THIS TITLE IS FROM OUR COMPUTER SCIENCE COLLECTION

Lisa MacLean, Editor

Momentum Press is one of the leading book publishers in the field of engineering, mathematics, health, and applied sciences. Momentum Press offers over 30 collections, including Aerospace, Biomedical, Civil, Environmental, Nanomaterials, Geotechnical, and many others.

Momentum Press is actively seeking collection editors as well as authors. For more information about becoming an MP author or collection editor, please visit http://www.momentumpress.net/contact

Announcing Digital Content Crafted by Librarians

Momentum Press offers digital content as authoritative treatments of advanced engineering topics by leaders in their field. Hosted on ebrary, MP provides practitioners, researchers, faculty, and students in engineering, science, and industry with innovative electronic content in sensors and controls engineering, advanced energy engineering, manufacturing, and materials science.

Momentum Press offers library-friendly terms:

- perpetual access for a one-time fee
- no subscriptions or access fees required
- unlimited concurrent usage permitted
- downloadable PDFs provided
- free MARC records included
- free trials

The **Momentum Press** digital library is very affordable, with no obligation to buy in future years.

For more information, please visit **www.momentumpress.net/library** or to set up a trial in the US, please contact **mpsales@globalepress.com**.

www.ingramcontent.com/pod-product-compliance
Lightning Source LLC
Chambersburg PA
CBHW070738220326
41598CB00024BA/3469